THE JIMMY BUFFETT
TRIVIA BOOK

THE JIMMY BUFFETT TRIVIA BOOK

501 Questions and Answers for Parrot Heads

Thomas Ryan

Citadel Press
Kensington Publishing Corp.
www.kensingtonbooks.com

This book is dedicated to Kimmy Buffett, Kathy Shedd,
and every single Parrot Head.

CITADEL PRESS books are published by

Kensington Publishing Corp.
850 Third Avenue
New York, NY 10022

All Kensington titles, imprints, and distributed lines are available at special quantity
discounts for bulk purchases for sales promotions, premiums, fund raising, educational,
or institutional use. Special book excerpts or customized printings can also be created
to fit specific needs. For details, write or phone the office of the Kensington special
sales manager: Kensington Publishing Corp., 850 Third Avenue, New York, NY 10022,
attn: Special Sales Department, phone 1-800-221-2647.

Kensington and the K logo Reg. U.S. Pat. & TM Office
Citadel Press is a trademark of Kensington Publishing Corp.

First printing 1998

10 9 8 7 6 5

Printed in the United States of America

Library of Congress Cataloging-in-Publication Data

Ryan, Thomas, 1958–
    The Jimmy Buffett trivia book : 501 questions and answers for
parrot heads / Thomas Ryan.
        p.   cm.
    "A Citadel Press book."
    ISBN 0-8065-1922-3 (pbk.)
    1. Buffett, Jimmy—Miscellanea.   I. Title.
ML420.B874R9   1997
782.42164′092—dc21   97–41402
    [B]   CIP
                                                               MN

CONTENTS

INTRODUCTION

The Jimmy Buffett Trivia Book questions more than you will ever need to know about the man *Rolling Stone* magazine has called "a human tourist attraction"...and yes, there will be a test afterward.

You just can't know enough about Jimmy Buffett. If you're already a fan, then you know exactly what I mean. If you don't know what I'm talking about, then it's high time you found out. Buffett has been a well-known singer-songwriter for over twenty-five years and his renown has grown to the point that he is no longer simply a pop artist. Nowadays, he is a cultural icon. More than any other artist of our time, Buffett represents a musical style that is uniquely his own, and the Parrot Heads have embodied his musical style and transformed it into a lifestyle. That is why the world can now be neatly divided into two halves—Parrot Heads and non-Parrot Heads. Either way you look at it, the man has affected your life. The quizzes contained in this book are designed to determine where you fit in the overall scheme of things.

The Jimmy Buffett Trivia Book is a collection of trivia questions on the various aspects of Buffett's career. The questions are divided into chronological chapters, each cover-ing a specific time period. Each section contains a forty-question trivia quiz on that portion of Jimmy Buffett's career and each quiz tends to get more difficult than those that precede it. For the technically challenged, there is a simple introductory quiz at the end of this section that will determine if you have prepared yourself adequately for the questions that follow. For those who already know too much, the last chapter concludes with a "final exam" of sorts, a one-hundred question brain-buster that is designed to trip up even the most thoroughly obsessive Parrot Head.

So then, are you ready to be tested? Are you an obsessed fan, a lunatic Parrot Head or just a casual listener? If you're serious, are you ready to delve into the minutest details of this singer-songwriter's career? Maybe you know Jimmy's middle name and his birthday, but do you know what that indecipherable scribble is on the inner sleeve of *Changes in Latitudes, Changes in Attitudes?* Maybe you know the lyrics to many of the *Songs You Know by Heart*, but are you equally familiar with the balance of his output? If so, then chances are excellent that *The Jimmy Buffett Trivia Book* will question more than you ever needed to know.

"What's all these crazy questions they're asking me?"

—Randy Newman
"Mama Told Me Not to Come"

An Introductory Quiz: Jimmy Buffett 101

Everybody's got to begin someplace, so here is where we will embark on our search for true Parrot Head fanatics. Following are a few questions with answers that should be known by anyone who thinks of themselves as a Parrot Head. Those who have a lot of experience at Parrot Head-ism should find this quiz a piece of cake. Friends and relatives of fanatics who are not yet convinced should begin here as well, in order to determine just how much of the Parrot Head disease has rubbed off on them.

The questions in this section are relatively tame, so this quiz should be used as a gauge to determine whether or not you have been indoctrinated. If you do well, then you are fully prepared to plunge ahead and see how well you do in the upcoming chapters, each with questions regarding the different stages of Jimmy Buffett's career (believe me, they won't be as simple as this quiz). If you do poorly, then you fall into one of two categories. Maybe you don't *want* to be a Parrot Head, and you just wanted to be sure that you were still unaffected and "safe." If that's the case, then congratulations on your failure. Now, if I were you, I would lock myself into a soundproof box and remain there for the rest of my days, because Jimmy Buffett, and *especially* the Parrot Heads, are not going to just up and disappear. Then, ask yourself: Do you want to spend the rest of your life running from something that is unavoidable?

You might as well face it. It's inevitable. Give it up! Succumb! On the other hand, maybe you really do want to be a Parrot Head, but just haven't had a chance to brush up on all of the stuff that you need to know. Well, if that's the case, don't lose heart. My first advice is, "Get thee to a Jimmy Buffett concert." Next, buy the records. Third, read a few of his stories. By then, you'll be thoroughly prepared to proceed through this book and check out all of the remarkable ephemera (i.e., useless information) that there is to be known, and realize that this is only a partial representation of the information that is out there.

Will your knowledge hold up under such intense scrutiny? We'll soon find out.

This quiz (as with every other other in this book with the exception of the one-hundred question final, or "ultimate" quiz) consists of forty questions. Each question is worth a total of five points. Answer them as honestly as you are able. Keep in mind that some questions may have more than one correct answer. If that's the case, you'll get points proportionate to the number of correct answers that you choose. Good luck.

INTRODUCTORY QUIZ

Q1.　Which of the following titles is not the name of a Jimmy Buffett album?
   a. *A White Sport Coat and a Pink Crustacean*
   b. *Last Mango in Paris*
   c. *Off to See the Lizard*
   d. *Sunburned Buns and Really Bad Puns*

Q2.　One of Jimmy's early '70s releases is titled *A1A*. What is "A1A"?
   a. His favorite brand of steak sauce
   b. The beach-access highway designation along Florida's Atlantic coast
   c. The highway designation for the main artery that connects all the Florida keys to the mainland
   d. A nautical heading for due south

Q3. What is the title of Jimmy Buffett's live double album, released in 1979?
  a. *Before the Beach*
  b. *You Had to Be There*
  c. *I'm Jimmy Buffett, and You're Not*
  d. *Feeding Frenzy*
  e. *Floridays*

Q4. Name the newsletter that Jimmy Buffett distributes to keep his fans informed and in touch.
  a. *Parrottalk*
  b. The *Banana Wind*
  c. The *Coconut Telegraph*
  d. The *Margaritaville Press*

Q5. What is the name of JB's record label?
  a. Iguana Records
  b. Margaritaville Records
  c. ABC/Dunhill
  d. Caribbean Soul

Q6. Who coined the term "Parrot Heads," anyway?
  a. Jimmy Buffett, of course
  b. Don Henley
  c. Timothy B. Schmit
  d. Jerry Garcia

Q7. True or False: Jimmy Buffett's birthday is also Christmas Day.

Q8. True or False: Jimmy Buffett owns a retail store in Miami, Florida that sells custom-made tropical clothing.

Q9. True or False: James Delaney Buffett III is the Head Parrot's full and proper name.

Jimmy Buffett concerts are famous for their audience participation, particularly in the audience's ability to sing along with virtually every song. Any fan worth his suntan ought to be able to complete the following lyrical phrases (in tune, of course, for 3 points each), and the song from whence it came (another 2 points):

Q10. "I like mine with lettuce and tomato…"

Q11. "Some people claim…"

The following four questions are simply to determine if you are in the appropriate spirit for a test like this:

Q12. Generally speaking, the audience at a typical Jimmy Buffett concert consists of
   a. partying teenagers
   b. partying grandmothers
   c. partying mid-life crisis victims
   d. anybody or anything with the "partying" adjective as a prefix.

Q13. Antidotes for severe Parrot Head-itis include
   a. a lifelong visit from your mother-in-law
   b. a tax audit
   c. working overtime on the weekend
   d. listening to anything by the Cure

Q14. Dangerous overdose material for severe Parrot Head-itis include
   a. hanging out for a week in the French Quarter of New Orleans, particularly Bourbon Street
   b. making the fourteenth pitcher of frozen drinks using any alcohol that is available (since you've long ago run out of the correct ingredients), in order to enhance your appreciation of the impending sunrise
   c. a beach party after midnight, attended by super-models
   d. a six-month "cruise to nowhere" aboard a party boat that is hosting a strippers' convention

Q15. Who won the 1996 World Series?
   a. The Chicago Cubs
   b. The New York Yankees
   c. The New York Mets
   d. Jimmy Buffett
   e. The Atlanta Braves

Q16. What are "Fins"?

   a. Those huge things on the back of a '63 Caddy

   b. Those terrifying things on the back of a great white shark

   c. Those terrifying things a normal guy grows when he turns into a land shark on Saturday night

   d. A strange ritual dance perfected by Parrot Heads and performed en masse at concerts until it looks like 18,000 drunken Radio City Rockettes moving in lopsided synchronization with each other

   e. A $10 bill

Q17. The Southern-most city in the continental U.S. is…

   a. San Antonio, Texas

   b. Miami, Florida

   c. San Diego, California

   d. Key West, Florida

Q18. Who is the accredited songwriter of "Why Don't We Get Drunk and Screw"?

   a. Jimmy Buffett

   b. Marvin Gardens

   c. Park Place

   d. Mr. Potato Head

Q19. What is the moniker that has been applied to the children of Parrot Heads?

   a. Parrot Droppings

   b. Conch Fritters

   c. Parakeets

   d. Bubba-babies

Q20. Here's one you ought to handle without difficulty. Finish the following phrase:

   "I've got a Caribbean soul I can barely control…"

Q21. Here's one that you might not even need "Buffett-knowledge" for: What TV game show is being parodied in the song "Door Number Three"?

   a. *The Price is Right*

   b. *The Gong Show*

   c. *Supermarket Sweep*
   d. *Let's Make a Deal*

Q22. "A Pirate Looks at Forty" is an aural portrait of
   a. Tom Corcoran
   b. Jimmy Buffett
   c. Phil Clark
   d. Tony Tarracino

Q23. What meal does Jimmy think would be just fine to eat each and every day of the year?
   a. Oysters and beer
   b. A cheeseburger and a cold draft beer
   c. Lobster and white wine
   d. Boiled shrimp and sponge cake

Q24. In the lyrics of the song "Boat Drinks," where is it that Jimmy needs to escape to?
   a. St. Thomas
   b. St. Bartolomey
   c. San Maarten
   d. St. John
   e. St. Somewhere

Q25. Where does the girl in the song "Fins" come from?
   a. New York
   b. Chicago
   c. Miami
   d. Cincinnati

Q26. In "Miss You So Badly," what female singer does Jimmy say that "There is just no one like her"?
   a. Loretta Lynn
   b. Patsy Cline
   c. Bessie Smith
   d. Billie Holiday

Q27. Can you pick the two instrumentals that were released by Jimmy Buffett and the Coral Reefer band?
   a. "Reggae Accident"
   b. "Dixie Diner"
   c. "Morris' Nightmare"

    d. "Banana Wind"

    e. "Barometer Soup"

Q28. Below are listed four consecutively released albums from the early eighties. Arrange them in their proper order of release, from earliest to latest.

    a. *One Particular Harbor*

    b. *Coconut Telegraph*

    c. *Riddles in the Sand*

    d. *Somewhere Over China*

Q29. On a similar note, match the album with the year of its release.

    a. *Volcano*   1. 1976

    b. *Changes in Latitudes,*   2. 1977
       Changes in Attitudes   3. 1978

    c. *Havana Daydreamin'*   4. 1979

    d. *Son of a Son of a Sailor*

Q30. Jimmy Buffett wrote one song for each of his two daughters and he mentions his son in another. From the following selection, choose the three songs that either mention or are specifically about one of his three children.

    a. "Delaney Talks to Statues"

    b. "False Echoes"

    c. "Growing Older but Not Up"

    d. "Come to the Moon"

    e. "Chanson Pour Les Petits Enfants"

    f. "Little Miss Magic"

    g. "Jolly Mon Sing"

Q31. Match the song title with the album that contains it.

    1. "Where's the Party"   a. *A White Sport Coat and a Pink Crustacean*

    2. "Makin' Music for Money"

    3. "The Great Filling Station Hold Up"   b. *Somewhere Over China*

    4. "Everybody's on the Run"   c. *Last Mango in Paris*

                         d. *A1A*

Q32. Which of the following songs does *not* appear on *Songs You Know by Heart?*
   a. "A Pirate Looks at Forty"
   b. "The Captain and the Kid"
   c. "Boat Drinks"
   d. "He Went to Paris"

Q33. At the onset of the nineties, Buffett was key in helping a friend of his be elected as Mayor of Key West. Who was this?
   a. Tom McGuane
   b. Phil Clark
   c. Tony Tarracino
   d. Bob Graham

Q34. In the mid-nineties, a deal was struck whereby the distribution for Margaritaville Records would be handled by a label other than MCA. Which record company now has that responsibility?
   a. Arista
   b. Sony
   c. Island
   d. ABC

Hmmm...for simple questions, these may be getting just a bit too tough for neophytes. Let's break it down a bit and simplify things again. Fill in the missing word from the following lyrics:

Q35. "Life and ink, they seem to run out at the same time, or so said my old friend the _____."

Q36. "Ia ora te natura, e mea arofa teie ao _____."

Q37. "'Monsieur, ou y'est le casino?' He spoke to the cabbie and smiled. The driver replied, 'veaux ou _____ ...'"

Oh, you would have preferred that my chosen quotes remained in English? Sorry, that didn't occur to me.

Q38. How about matching the following song titles with the album that contains the original (or first-released) recording?

a.	"God's Own Drunk"	1.	*Banana Wind*
b.	"Migration"	2.	*A1A*
c.	"Defying Gravity"	3.	*Living and Dying in*
d.	"Banana Republics"		*³/₄ Time*
e.	"Dixie Diner"	4.	*You Had to Be There*
f.	"The Captain and the Kid"	5.	*Last Mango in Paris*
		6.	*Christmas Island*
g.	"Jolly Mon Sing"	7.	*Down to Earth*
h.	"Schoolboy Heart"	8.	*Havana Daydreamin'*
i.	"Mele Kalikimaka"	9.	*Changes in Latitudes,*
j.	"Apocalypso"		*Changes in Attitudes*
		10.	*Fruitcakes*

Q39. How many of Buffett's album titles (excluding soundtracks) are also the title of a song that is contained on the album?
   a. 9
   b. 12
   c. 15
   d. 19

Q40. Finally, here's your last question. Margaritaville is...
   a. a restaurant
   b. a nightclub
   c. a souvenir shop
   d. an undiscovered island paradise
   e. a song title
   f. a record label
   g. a state of mind

ANSWERS

A1.   c. "Sunburned Buns and Really Bad Puns" is not the name of a Jimmy Buffett album, but he can use it if he likes.

A2.   b, although I'll bet that a few Parrot Heads picked c. The main artery that connects the Florida Keys is Highway 1. 'A1A' runs for the entire length of Florida's eastern coast, until it ends abruptly in Miami. This "beach access" designation reappears on a short run of highway along the southeast coast of Key West—that's where the album photos were taken. As an interesting aside, Florida's highway department was less than pleased with the outcome of such recognition, when over-zealous fans began to swipe the signs with such regularity that they could no longer afford to keep installing new replacements. Nevertheless, in 1981, Florida Governor Bob Graham bestowed Jimmy with an "A1A" plaque, as a token of thanks for promoting Florida tourism (much to Jimmy's chagrin, I'm sure).

A3. b. *You Had to Be There*

A4. c. The *Coconut Telegraph*

A5. a. The Iguanas are a New Orleans–based band that happen to record on Margaritaville. 0 points

b. Margaritaville Records is correct. 5 points

c. Dunhill/ABC was the label that launched Jimmy's career, but he doesn't own it (at least not yet). Close counts, though, so take 2 points.

d. Caribbean Soul is the name of Jimmy's clothing line, not his record label. 0 points

A6. c. Timothy B. Schmit, ex-member of Poco, an Eagle, and sometime member of Jimmy Buffett's Coral Reefer band, came up with the term when joking that the audience looked like Deadheads, only with crazier, tropical clothing ("They're not Deadheads, they're…*Parrot Heads!*").

A7. True. Jimmy Buffett was born on Christmas Day, December 25, 1946.

A8. False. It's in Key West, Florida, with another in New Orleans, Louisiana (everything else is true, though).

A9. False, but this question might even fool a few dedicated fans, because other publications have claimed this to be his name. His *grandfather's* name was James Delaney Buffett and his father was James D. Buffett, Jr. but Jimmy's full name is James William Buffett (and he isn't "III" since his full name is different from his immediate male predecessors).

Thought for the day: Jimmy was raised as a Catholic, which means that he probably took a confirmation name. Could it have been Delaney?

A10. "...Heinz 57 and French-fried potatoes" (3 points) from "Cheeseburger in Paradise" (2 points)

A11. "...that there's a woman to blame, but I know it's my own damn fault," or "it could be my fault" or "it's nobody's fault" (3 points), from "Margaritaville" (2 points). If you didn't get *this* one, then there exists only one of two possibilities. Either 1) you don't have a clue why this book is in your lap, or 2) your life must be like a Cheech and Chong movie ("That show was *awesome*, man. What's his name again?"). I'll bet every Parrot Head has had their share of these types of characters roaming (weaving, actually) around the parking lot before show time, only to find them face down in the Porta Potti three hours later.

A12. a through c are all acceptable, but d is the best answer. Take 4 points for either a through c, and take 5 if you answered d.

A13. All of the above. Take 1 point for each, and 5 points if you were clever enough to pick all of them.

A14. All of the above. Take 1 point for each, and 5 points if you were clever enough to pick all of them. New Orleans' Bourbon Street, by the way, is the meeting place for the annual Parrot Head "Meeting of the Minds" gathering. It takes place during the first week of November—don't say I didn't warn you.

A15. Just checking. You might have noticed that this question has absolutely nothing to do with Jimmy Buffett. Well, it's here because I want to be sure that you realize the importance of having some sort of existence away from all of this. It's important to have your own identity, right? I mean, Jimmy's great and all, but the world's a big, complicated place. That being said, take 5 points if you answered d (take 5 if you answered b, too, since that *is* technically the right answer).

A16. This is a "gimme," since all answers are technically correct, and Buffett intimates all of them, except perhaps the '63 Caddy. The song "Fins" makes reference to how men can often prowl through the night like a shark on the hunt, and the "fins" dance is a regular feature at live concerts. As for the $10 bill reference, Buffett uses the term this way himself in the lyrics to "I Heard I Was in Town" ("when a full tank (of gas) was only a fin").

A17. d. I mean, why else would this question be in a Jimmy Buffett trivia test?

A18. b. Marvin Gardens, as you probably already know, is a piece of yellow real estate in the board game Monopoly.

A19. c. for God's sake.

A20. "…and some Texas hidden here in my heart."

A21. d

A22. c

A23. According to the lyrics of "Tin Cup Chalice," "Give me oysters and beer for dinner every day of the year and I'll be fine."

A24. e

A25. d

A26. b. He would eventually cover one of Patsy Cline's biggest hits. Interestingly, Buffett would perform his version of "She's Got You" (from *Fruitcakes*) without changing the gender.

A27. b and d

A28. b (1981), d (1982), a (1983), and c (1984).

A29. a-4, b-2, c-1 and d-3. Also, Jimmy's first live album, *You Had to Be There,* was released in 1978.

A30. a, b, and f. "Little Miss Magic" is written for Savannah Jane, "Delaney Talks to Statues" is written for Sarah Delaney, and "False Echoes" mentions his son, Cameron Marley.

A31. 1-b, 2-d, 3-a, and 4-c. All songs, by the way, are the lead-off tracks of their respective albums.

A32. b. Although all of the songs on Buffett's greatest hits collection are culled from his '70s releases, nothing was taken from *Havana Daydreamin'*.

A33. c. Tony Tarracino owned and operated Captain Tony's Saloon and had continually run for the post of mayor, only to fail time after time. This time around, Buffett gave his campaign a push by lobbying for the Key West legend, contributing to Captain Tony being elected to the office. Buffett discusses this before launching into "Last Mango in Paris" on the *Feeding Frenzy* album.

A34. c

A35. ...squid (get it? squid-ink? ink? squid? get it?). This is excerpted from "If I Could Just Get It on Paper," from *Somewhere Over China*.

A36. "...nei." This is excerpted from the sing-along chorus of "One Particular Harbor." Spelling doesn't count, so if you wrote "nay" or "nae," that'll do just fine.

A37. "...nouveaux." Pardon my French, but spelling doesn't count here, either (especially since I haven't a clue about the correct French spelling anyway).

A38. a-3, b-2, c-8, d-9, e-4, f-7, g-5, h-1, i-6, j-10. Take 1 point for every two matches (5 points max).

A39. c. They are 1) *High Cumberland Jubilee*, 2) *Havana Daydreamin'*, 3) *Changes in Latitudes, Changes in Attitudes*, 4) *Son of a Son of a Sailor*, 5) *Volcano*, 6) *Coconut Telegraph*, 7) *Somewhere Over China*, 8) *One Particular Harbor*, 9) *Last Mango in Paris*, 10) *Floridays*, 11) *Off to See the Lizard*, 12) *Fruitcakes*, 13) *Barometer Soup*, 14) *Banana Wind*, and 15) *Christmas Island*.

A40. A freebie. All answers were correct, so take 5 points.

Score Results

So, how did you do? Sorry about the occasional trick question, especially so early in the proceedings (this *is* supposed to be the easy section, after all), but you might as well get used to it because in upcoming sections I'll be deliberately trying to stump you. You probably didn't do so bad anyway. Let's review your score.

0–50 points—You must have picked this book up accidentally, thinking it was a recipe book for *buffets*. Go back to where you bought it, and maybe they'll let you exchange it for a copy of *The Poor Speller's Cookbook*.

51–100 points—I guess you only go to the shows because your girl- or boyfriend goes all the time, and the *real* reason you're there is because you're afraid of what trouble they might get themselves into if you *didn't* go. You're a good sport, though, and if you study the rest of this book and improve your skills in Buffett-ology, I can almost guarantee that it will improve your love life immeasurably. Don't thank me, thank Jimmy.

101–150 points—You're an aspiring party master, but you lack the experience needed to be a true, virtuoso celebrator. Maybe now you invite people over to play board games, only to realize when they arrive that you once again forgot to make ice. Well, don't worry. This book is for you, bub. By the time we're done with you, you'll be a first-class party machine, rocking out at poolside with your own icemaker, ice crusher, *and* industrial strength turbo-blender.

151–200 points—So, you are already something of a pro in Buffett-ology and probably think this quiz was kid's stuff. You probably also think that you'll be able to tear your way through the rest of the book, too. You're a real know-it-all, aren't you? Well, let's just see how much you do know. The following sections are designed to test your mettle. We'll know soon enough whether or not you can be humbled.

I

The Early Years

The first quiz contains questions based on Jimmy Buffett's life "before the beach," i.e., from his grandfather's legacy to the completion of his contractual obligation with Barnaby Records. "What is Barnaby Records?" you ask. Hmm. While you might be familiar with a few of Buffett's legendary tales from his youth, this section also covers some of Buffett's most obscure music, so proceed at your own risk. At a minimum, I recommend that you familiarize yourself with Margaritaville Records' compilation of Jimmy Buffett's early years, entitled *Before the Beach*, before you proceed any further. If you think you're prepared, then dig in. The albums that are covered in this section include

Down to Earth	1970
High Cumberland Jubilee	1971 (unreleased until 1976)

Both albums are currently out of print. Most of the material that originally appeared on these albums is presently available on *Before the Beach*—Margaritaville Records MCAD-10823, released in 1993.

QUIZ: THE EARLY YEARS

Now, let's see how much you know. You wouldn't have come this far if you didn't already consider yourself a fan, so this test should accurately gauge the depth of your dedication, particularly since it focuses on a time period that is often overlooked by many fans. Remember, each of the following forty questions are worth a total of five points each. If a question is complex, the answer will provide you with the correct method to assess your point score for that particular question. Understand? All right then, let's go.

Q1. What classic comedian passed away on the exact day of Jimmy Buffett's birth?
   a. Harpo Marx
   b. W. C. Fields
   c. Chico Marx
   d. Charlie Chaplin
   e. Buster Keaton

Q2. What was Jimmy Buffett's occupation before he became the world's most well-known and laid-back singer-sailor-songwriter?
   a. He was a tax consultant for his Uncle Warren.
   b. He sold vacuum cleaners door to door.
   c. He worked as a journalist for *Billboard* magazine.
   d. He was a librarian.

Q3. Which two of the following songs were included on the original *Down to Earth* album, but were deleted from the re-release package, *Before the Beach?*
   a. "The Christian?"
   b. "Ain't He a Genius"
   c. "I Can't Be Your Hero Today"
   d. "A Mile High in Denver"
   e. "Richard Frost"

Q4. Who was a major partner of Jimmy Buffett's first record label, Barnaby Records?
   a. Pat Boone
   b. Perry Como

    c. Andy Williams

    d. Sid Vicious

Q5. What was the title of Jimmy's first single on Barnaby Records? (Sorry, no multiple choice here—either you know it, or you don't.) To be nice about this, I'm only looking for the A-side.

Q6. Barnaby was a new label when Jimmy signed on. In fact, there was only one single released by Barnaby before Jimmy's. What was that single, and by whom?

    a. "Can't Get Used to Losing You"—Andy Williams

    b. "Everything is Beautiful"—Ray Stevens

    c. "Ahab the Arab"—Ray Stevens

    d. "I Gotcha"—Joe Tex

Q7. What song on *Before the Beach* did not previously make an appearance on either *Down to Earth* or *High Cumberland Jubilee?*

    a. "High Cumberland Jubilee"

    b. "Ace"

    c. "England"

    d. "Cumberland High Dilemma"

Q8. Jimmy Buffett shares writing credits on more than half of the songs that appear on the *High Cumberland Jubilee* album. Who was his cowriter in those days?

    a. Michael Utley

    b. Buzz Cason

    c. Travis Turk

    d. Greg "Fingers" Taylor

Q9. What is the parenthetical title of "God Don't Own a Car"?

    a. (But His Lear Jet's Pretty Nice)

    b. (No Wheels)

    c. (So Why Don't We Give Him a Ride?)

    d. (I Guess I'm Not Alone)

    e. (He'd Rather Take the Bus)

Q10. Match the following four lyrics with the song that contains them.

    a. "He's got the brains of Einstein and the brawn of Mr. Clean"

    b. "His virtue was sheer poverty, his vice was reading plays"
    c. "You tell your mother that you love another"
    d. "Exciting all the fools who pay to see the naked lady in our yard"
    1. "The Hang-Out Gang"
    2. "Travellin' Clean"
    3. "Ain't He a Genius"
    4. "Captain America"

Q11. What is the full (first and last) name of Jimmy's boss at *Billboard* magazine? (Hint: he had the same last name as the guy who sang "Moon River.")
    a. Bill Como
    b. Andy Wiliams
    c. Perry Bennett
    d. Bill Williams

In questions 12–15, finish the following lyrics (5 points each):

Q12. "I have been out wandering, I have traveled far. One conclusion I have made is..."

Q13. "The world was just a day away..."

Q14. "Nothing here is different. Nothing's changed at all..."

Q15. "Somebody told me the last word they heard her say was..."

Q16. What is the familial connection between Jimmy Buffett and *Mutiny on the Bounty?*
    a. His grandfather played the minor role of a deckhand in the 1930s film version, starring Clark Gable and Charles Laughton.
    b. His father played the minor role of a deckhand in the 1962 film version, starring Marlon Brando and Trevor Howard.
    c. A distant English-born relative named John Buffett took up residence on a south seas speck of land called Pitcairn's Island, where the surviving mutineers had settled a quarter-century earlier.

   d. A distant relative named John Buffett was among the surviving *Bounty* mutineers who spent the remainder of their days on Pitcairn's Island.

Q17. Which of the following has Jimmy Buffett claimed as a childhood hero?
   a. Jean Lafitte
   b. Captain Queeg
   c. Captain Hook
   d. Captain Bligh

Q18. Before he began his solo career in earnest, JB worked temporarily with a band that recorded knock-offs of popular hits. What was the name of this group?
   a. The Now Generation
   b. The Upstairs Alliance
   c. The Peanut Butter Conspiracy
   d. K - Tel Presents!

Q19. What was the original Spanish name for Key West?
   a. Cayo Hueso
   b. Huevos Ranchero
   c. Nuevo Huevo
   d. Cayo Nuevo

Q20. Jimmy Buffett is prominently featured in a black and white photo on the front cover of this 1972 Buddah records release, his guitar propped upright between his legs, wearing a "Ripple" T-shirt. The album is
   a. Jerry Jeff Walker—*Walker's Collectibles*
   b. John Prine—*Sweet Revenge*
   c. Steve Goodman—*Somebody Else's Troubles*
   d. David Bowie—*Ziggy Stardust and the Spiders From Mars*

Q21. Which of the following are *not* credited as drummers on the *Down to Earth* collection?
   a. Paul Tabet
   b. Tarvis Turk
   c. Karl Himmel
   d. Buzz Cason

Q22. What is Jimmy Buffett's mom's maiden name?
   a. Moss
   b. Walker
   c. Peets
   d. Petitte

Q23. Jimmy Buffett was born at the Jackson County Memorial Hospital, located just outside of Pascagoula, Mississippi on Christmas Day, 1946. Shortly afterward, the family relocated to...
   a. Jackson, Mississippi
   b. St. Somewhere, the Caribbean
   c. Arlington, Virginia
   d. Mobile, Alabama

Q24. Jimmy's grandfather originally hails from
   a. Scandinavia
   b. England
   c. Nova Scotia
   d. Mississippi

Q25. What is the name of Jimmy's paternal uncle?
   a. Billy
   b. Jimmy
   c. Delaney
   d. Marley

Q26. Jimmy's college "career" consisted of a few minor changes in latitudes. For a short while, he attended both Auburn University and Pearl River Junior College. Eventually, he would move on once more, obtaining his degree in journalism and history from what institute of higher learning?

Q27. Jimmy's got two sisters. Can you name at least one of them?

Q28. Jimmy got married rather quickly after leaving college. What was his first wife's name (her first name will suffice)?

OK, let's complete a few more lyrical phrases. This time, I'll give you the title and you complete the line that follows it. Each of the next two questions are worth five points each.

Q29. "Ellis Dee..."

Q30. "Ace..."

Q31. In what year did Jimmy complete his college education?
 a. 1967
 b. 1968
 c. 1969
 d. 1970

Q32. According to legend, Jimmy's infamous debut album, *Down to Earth*, is rumored to have sold how many copies?
 a. 37
 b. 374
 c. 3,740
 d. 33,740

Q33. The lead-off track on *Down to Earth* is...
 a. "Ellis Dee"
 b. "The Christian?"
 c. "Ace"
 d. "The Captain and the Kid"

Q34. Which of the folowing characters are *not* mentioned in the song "Captain America"?
 a. Einstein
 b. Mister Clean
 c. The Lone Ranger
 d. Tarzan

Q35. True or False—Jimmy Buffett's first-ever mention of his future wife Jane Slagsvol occurs on "Turnabout," with the line "While I tell you to your face how I really feel, you're not real, Lady Jane."

Q36. Which of the following songs lapses into a bar or two of "Camptown Ladies"?
 a. "Death Valley Lives"
 b. "The Hang-Out Gang"

   c. "I Can't Be Your Hero Today"
   d. "Rockefeller Square"

Q37. The front cover of the *Before the Beach* collection features a photograph of Buffett sitting on the hood of an old Packard. What does the license plate read?
   a. Goin South
   b. Flying Lady
   c. Highway Lady
   d. Mrs Bojangles

Q38. Who owned the Packard?

Q39. Buffett's liner notes on *Before the Beach* begin with which of the following phrases?
   a. So where were you when I released this stuff the first time around?
   b. These are the songs I've been trying to warn you about.
   c. These are the songs your parents warned you about.
   d. These are the songs that your parents never heard, so couldn't have warned you about.

Q40. Match the character with the song he or she appears in (one song title is used twice):
   a. Bucky Beaver   1. "Cumberland High Dilemma"
   b. Sarah   2. "I Can't Be Your Hero Today"
   c. Koochie   3. "Rockefeller Square"
   d. Holly   4. "The Hang-Out Gang"
   e. Tracy   5. "Death Valley Lives"
   f. Rocky   6. "Livingston's Gone to Texas"
   g. Jane

QUIZ ANSWERS

A1.   a. Nope. Harpo (real name Arthur) died in 1964. Jimmy was born in 1946. 0 points

b. Yes. W. C. Fields died on Christmas day, 1946, in perfect keeping with his comedic persona as the man most likely to ruin the party. He was 66 years old when his nose went out. 5 points

c. No. Chico died in 1961. 0 points

d. No, but coincidentally, the date of Charlie Chaplin's death also happened to be on Christmas Day (this is

getting spooky). He died in 1977, at the ripe old age of 88.
You can take 1 point for getting the day right, at least.
e. No. Buster Keaton passed away in 1965. He was 70
years old. 0 points

A2.   c. From his former incarnation as a journalist (he was
actually a staff reporter at *Billboard* magazine), Jimmy
Buffett may have developed the knack of structuring his
songs as interesting and literate stories that keep his
audience enraptured, even after repeated listenings. By
the way, could you ever in a million years imagine Jimmy
as a librarian?

A3.   a and b. Either because they were considered expendable
or because of copyright difficulties, "The Christian?" and
"Ain't He a Genius" were not included in the *Before the
Beach* compilation of Jimmy Buffett's first two albums,
Down to Earth and *Highland Cumberland Jubilee*. Give
yourself 2 points for one correct, 5 points for both.
c or d. Wrong. Both are on the album. 0 points
e. "Richard Frost" was deleted from *Before the Beach*, but
it wasn't included on the original *Down to Earth* album,
either. If you haven't heard it, it's a fairly nondescript
country-styled tune with a verse that bears a strong
resemblance to that of "Come Monday." Other than its
original appearance as the B-side of "The Christian?" it
only appeared on subsequent rerelease packages issued by
Barnaby. You were half right if you picked it, though, so
take 1 point.

A4.   c. Barnaby Records was owned by mellow crooner Andy
Williams, the man who, besides unsuccessfully trying to
introduce Jimmy Buffett to the world, had given us the
Osmond Brothers. 5 points

A5.   "The Christian?" (with question mark intact) was the title
of Jimmy's first single. 5 points

A6.   b. The first single release on Barnaby Records was "Everything Is Beautiful" by Ray Stevens (Barnaby no. 2011).
This went on to become a number one hit in the spring of

1970, making the miserable performance of Jimmy's first single (Barnaby no. 2013) that much more poignant.

A7. d

A8. b. 5 points. Buzz Cason got cowriting credits on "Rockefeller Square," "Bend a Little," "England," "The Hang-Out Gang," "God Don't Own a Car" and "High Cumberland Jubilee," (as well as the added track, "Cumberland High Dilemma"). He also played keyboards on the album.

A9. b. The song's full title is "God Don't Own a Car (No Wheels)." 5 points. If you picked e (He'd Rather Take the Bus), take 2 points, since that is from the song's lyrics and it shows that you probably know the song.

A10. a-4, b-3, c-2, d-1. 5 points if all are right, or 1 point for each correct match

A11. d

A12. "God don't own a car"

A13. "for the Captain and the kid"

A14. "Livingston's gone to Texas. They say he had a ball" (or "The snow's about to fall")

A15. "England"

A16. c. John Buffett was a crew member on an English vessel that journeyed to Pitcairn's Island. He was so impressed with the place that he requested permission to stay and help with "Westernization" of the native population, which was granted.

A17. a. Lafitte was a Caribbean "gentleman" pirate (i.e., he was accepted in various social circles, particularly in New Orleans) who made a temporary pact with Colonel Andrew Jackson to help "catch the bloody British in the town of New Orleans" (quoted phrase is a lyrical excerpt from Johnny Horton's early sixties hit single, "The Battle of New Orleans." Parenthetically, Horton would die in a car crash soon after the record's release). If you picked b or c, you're watching too much television (Captain Queeg was a character protrayed by Humphrey Bogart in *The Caine*

Mutiny and Captain Hook is from Peter Pan!). Captain Bligh (choice d) was the feared and supposedly tyrannical captain of the MSS *Bounty*.

A18. It was a, the Now Generation, a painfully unhip name, considering that the '60s were just about over. They released two albums with Jimmy, "Come Together" and "Hits Are Our Business." Each album featured Jimmy in the group photo cover shot. b was his New Orleans band and since they performed mostly covers, I'll give you two points if you chose them instead. As for c, there really was a band named the Peanut Butter Conspiracy, who had a regional west coast hit in the sixties called "It's a Happening Thing" (sounds like a good song title for the Now Generation, actually). As a Buffett fan, you must be inured to bad puns for album titles, so you probably won't moan in agony when I tell you that their album was called *The Peanut Butter Conspiracy is Spreading*.

A19. a (b happens to be a Spanish egg dish while c means "new egg" in Spanish). Cayo Hueso (pronounced KI-yo hoo-WA-so) means "island of bones" because the remains of ancient American Indians were found unburied on the beaches. Phonetically, you might notice that it is quite similar to the English name Key West.

A20. c. Something that longtime fans might find very interesting about this release are the liner notes that appear on the back cover, as follows: "The people on the front cover are Earl Pionke, John Prine, *Marvin Gardens*, Nancy Goodman, Miss Jesse Goodman, Steve Goodman, Fred Holstein, Edward Mark Holstein." Marvin Gardens gets no instrumental credits on the record. Nor does his alter ego, Jimmy Buffett.

A21. d

A22. c. Peets was both her maiden name and her "nickname."

A23. d. Mobile was a little more than an hour's drive away from Pascagoula and near the shipyards where Jimmy's father would go to work.

A24. c. At the age of fifteen, Jimmy's grandfather ran away from home and began his lifelong obsession with the sea. He would eventually settle down in Pascagoula, Mississippi, making Cuba and New Orleans regular destinations during his voyages.

A25. a. Jimmy's Uncle Billy is immortalized in his *Tales From Margaritaville* collection of short stories and in the song "Pascagoula Run," both of which concern themselves with a wild eye opener of an evening that the teenaged Jimmy spent in the company of his uncle. James Delaney is the name of Jimmy's father *and* grandfather. Marley is the middle name of Buffett's son, Cameron Marley.

A26. The University of Southern Mississippi (USM)

A27. Loraine Marie (Lori) and Lucy Ann (Lucy)

A28. Margie, or Margaret (Washichek)

A29. "…ain't free like you and me." By the way, I assume that everybody has made the rather obvious and silly phonetical connection between "Ellis Dee" and the hallucinogenic drug LSD? I thought so.

A30. "…can't read and Ace can't write"

A31. c

A32. b

A33. b

A34. d. Tarzan *does* happen to be mentioned later in the album during "I Can't be Your Hero Today," though.

A35. False, false, false. First of all, Jimmy was just recently married to his first wife at this time. Secondly, he hadn't yet gone to Key West, where he would eventually meet up with Jane a few years later—this is obviously a reference to another "Lady Jane." Lastly, this line is from "I Can't Be Your Hero Today," not "Turnabout."

A36. d

A37. b

A38. Jerry Jeff Walker

A39. c, although it probably should have been d.

A40. a-1, a-2, d-3, f-4, e-5, c-6, b-7. Take five points for all correct answers, or take one point for each correct match (no more than five points, though).

Score Results

10–50 points—You mean you haven't exchanged this book for a cookbook yet? Jeesh, what are you waiting for? Now, it's too late, since you probably wrote all over the pages while trying to figure out what these questions had to do with food. At this point, you might as well stick it out and finish the book, but go out and buy a few Jimmy Buffett records first!

51–100 points—You're still hanging in there, eh? Well, maybe your heart isn't in it yet, but if you scored over 50, then you're probably more interested in Jimmy Buffett than you are letting on. That's right, if you scored in this range, then it unequivocally proves that you are a closet Parrot Head.

101–160 points—Not bad at all, especially since this section tests your knowledge of a time that most Buffett afficionados are least familiar with. Pat yourself on the back, and move on.

161–200 points—They don't make questions too tough for you, do they? I went easy on you, though (I could have gotten really obscure in the lyric section, for example. I'll bet that would have tripped you up). Well, before you start thinking that this whole test thing is going to be a piece of cake, hang on, because upcoming sections may not be quite as considerate.

2

The Early Seventies

In the early seventies, Jimmy Buffett made a trip to Key West that would influence him profoundly and set the standard for practically everything else that followed. Playing the role of the local troubador, his songwriting flourished and his appeal was strengthened enough for him to make a fresh start with another record label. When the Nashville branch of ABC Records beckoned, Buffett heeded the call. With his latest batch of songs, he would unselfconsciously create a new style of music that came to be known as "Gulf-Western." The quiz contained in this section concerns itself with the period beginning with his trip to Key West and ends in 1974. If you're a fan then you ought to be intimately familiar with the classic albums released during these years. They are

A White Sport Coat and a Pink Crustacean	1973
Living and Dying in ³/₄ Time	1974
"Rancho Deluxe" Motion Picture Soundtrack	1975*
A1A	1974

*(Although recorded in 1974, the release was delayed until 1975.)

AND NOW, THE QUIZ

Q1. I've witnessed it with my own eyes; legions of Parrot Heads can sing this all the way through, at the top of their lungs. Just take me to the end of the first chorus:
"I really do..."

Q2. What brand of beer can be seen resting on the arm of the beach chair in the cover photo for the *A1A* album (no peeking!)?
  a. Heineken (a greenie)
  b. Budweiser
  c. Michelob
  d. Corona

Q3. Which of the following actors and actresses starred in *Rancho Deluxe?* Choose as many as you think is correct.
  a. Jeff Bridges
  b. Sam Waterston
  c. Elizabeth Ashley
  d. Slim Pickens
  e. Harry Dean Stanton

Q4. In this Tom McGuane–scripted western, what is the name of the Montana ranch that is being plagued by rustlers?
  a. The B Bar Lazy T Ranch
  b. The Double R Bar Ranch
  c. The Bar and Grill Ranch
  d. Rancho Deluxe

Q5. Although his appearance onscreen is quite short in *Rancho Deluxe*, you do get a chance to see a very young Jimmy Buffett performing live with a few other bandmembers. In this scene, who is playing mandolin?
  a. Michael Utley
  b. Tom McGuane
  c. Bill Monroe
  d. Levon Helm

Q6. In his early solo days in Key West, Jimmy would occasionally introduce his imaginary back-up band as the "Coral

Reefers," a marijuana-inspired pun that the audience had no trouble understanding. Then, he would introduce each fictional player, one at a time. Take one point for each fictitious player that you can name, and five points if you name all four.

Q7. Who wrote the introductory liner notes to *A White Sport Coat and a Pink Crustacean?*
   a. Jerry Jeff Walker
   b. Tom McGuane
   c. Marty Robbins
   d. Jimmy did them himself

Q8. In those same liner notes, Jimmy is considered as a composite of which of the following couplets?
   a. Lefty Frizell and Desi Arnaz
   b. Hank Williams and Xavier Cougat
   c. James Taylor and Lucille Ball
   d. Gordon Lightfoot and Little Richard
   e. Carmen Miranda and Peter Lorre

Q9. What song from *White Sport Coat* did JB cowrite with Jerry Jeff Walker?
   a. "Why Don't We Get Drunk"
   b. "The Great Filling Station Hold Up"
   c. "Railroad Lady"
   d. "Death of an Unpopular Poet"

Q10. How many of *Living and Dying in* ³/₄ *Time*'s eleven songs were not written exclusively by Jimmy?
   a. None
   b. Two
   c. Three
   d. All but two

Q11. How many songs on *Living and Dying in* ³/₄ *Time* are actually written in ³/₄ time?
   a. That's a stupid question. All of them, obviously.
   b. No, no, no, noooo! He's only fooling around! None of them are in ³/₄ time.
   c. I dunno. Only one, I think.
   d. What the heck is ³/₄ time?

Q12. How many of *A1A*'s ten songs were not written by Jimmy?
 a. Two
 b. Three
 c. Four
 d. Five

Q13. What is Jimmy's choice of footwear in "Come Monday"?
 a. Flip-flops
 b. Hiking boots
 c. Hush Puppies
 d. High heels
 e. Tennis shoes

In questions 14 and 15, since crossing paths with Jimmy, Buford Pusser's legend has entered the realm of Parrot Heads. For this reason, then, I pose the following two questions.

Q14. Who sings the theme song to *Walking Tall?*
 a. Johnny Cash
 b. Johnny Mathis
 c. Jimmy Buffett
 d. Jerry Jeff Walker

Q15. Who plays Buford Pusser in the first *Walking Tall* movie?
 a. Clint Eastwood
 b. Burt Reynolds
 c. Joe Dan Baker
 d. Terry Bradshaw

Q16. What songs were on Jimmy's first single for ABC Records (both sides, please)?
 a. "Why Don't We Get Drunk" b/w "They Don't Dance Like Carmen No More"
 b. "Why Don't We Get Drunk" b/w "Grapefruit—Juicy Fruit"
 c. "The Great Filling Station Hold Up" b/w "They Don't Dance Like Carmen No More"
 d. "The Great Filling Station Hold Up" b/w "Why Don't We Get Drunk"

Q17. On what album (2 points) and song (3 points) does Jimmy sing about "living and dying in three-quarter time" (sorry, no multiple choice here)?

Q18. No doubt about it, *A1A* is what is called a "lifestyles" album. For example, Jimmy wrote seven songs on the album by himself. How many of these seven songs mention alcohol or drinking?
   a. Three
   b. Four
   c. Five
   d. Six

Q19. What less than complimentary phrase does Jimmy use on the liner notes of *A1A* to describe Miami?
   a. Octegenarian magnet
   b. Geriatric County
   c. Wrinkle City
   d. Geezer Beach

Q20. A two-part question: In the song "The Great Filling Station Hold Up," where did the drunken partners in crime decide to lay low (3 points) and what was it (2 points)?
   a. The Diamond   1. a bar
   b. The Krystal   2. a fast-food joint
   c. White Castle   3. a porno movie house
   d. Shoney's   4. a drive-in

Q21. In "The Great Filling Station Hold Up," how much gas does the singer request before pulling off his great heist?
   a. Two bucks' worth
   b. A fin
   c. A dollar
   d. Fifty cents

For the next few questions, I'll provide the title. You provide the accompanying couplet (i.e., the lyrics before or after the title)

Q22. "She's a railroad lady..."

Q23. "Grapefruit..."

Q24. "...Brahma Fear."

Q25. In "He Went to Paris," can you name the wife and child of the song's subject?

Q26. What song mentions "a fat barmaid, a cowboy, and a dog"?
    a. "Brahma Fear"
    b. "The Wino and I Know"
    c. "Ringling Ringling"
    d. "Left Me With a Nail to Drive"

Q27. After "He Went to Paris," "he" then went to England. What did he do while in England?
    a. Wrote a novel
    b. Fought as a mercenary
    c. Learned to dance
    d. Played the piano

Q28. In what song does Buffett invoke his audience during the instrumental break with "Ladies' choice, everybody now"?
    a. "Grapefruit—Juicy Fruit"
    b. "The Great Filling Station Hold Up"
    c. "The Peanut Butter Conspiracy"
    d. "Saxophones"

Q29. Match the song with the character(s) that appear in them. Hint: Certain song titles may be used more than once, others not at all.
    1. Billy Voltaire   a. "Nautical Wheelers"
    2. Meritta   b. "Havana Daydreamin'"
    3. Shrimper Dan   c. "The Peanut Butter Conspiracy"
    4. Ricky   d. "Cuban Crime of Passion"

Q30. On *White Sport Coat and a Pink Crustacean*, Buffett sings "'Cause they don't dance like Carmen no more. She and old Cougie, my what a pair." Who are Carmen and Cougie?

Q31. I guess we all know that "God's own truck" was a faded turquoise green, but do you know what color Jimmy's bicycle was in the Key West days?

For questions 32–35, name the songs that contain the following lyrics:

Q32. "She can eat her own weight up in crabmeat."

Q33. "He left all his royalties to Spooner his old hound."

Q34. "Remember that time in Montana you said there'd be no room for doubt?"

Q35. "Well, there's a whorehouse on the edge of town for anybody able to screw."

Q36. Can you name at least three characters whose name Buffett evokes in the lyrics to "Pencil Thin Mustache'?

Q37. Since we're on threes, the *Rancho Deluxe* soundtrack contains six instrumentals. Can you name at least three of them?

In the interest of mercy, we'll return to multiple choice for the balance of this quiz:

Q38. One of the *Rancho Deluxe* songs that does feature vocals is sung by someone other than Buffett. What song is that?
  a. "Can't Remember Where I Slept Last Night"
  b. "Countin' the Cows Every Day"
  c. "Cattle Truckin'"
  d. "Left Me With a Nail to Drive"

Q39. The alcohol-induced incident that involved a dangerous (but in retrospect, hilarious) confrontation between Jimmy Buffett and the legendary Southern sheriff Buford Pusser, involving fistfuls of hair, a hand being stabbed with a bic pen, and a tire iron, took place in the parking lot of Roger Miller's King of the Road Hotel. What band member was unfortunate enough to get personally involved in this mess?
  a. Sammy Creason
  b. Fingers Taylor
  c. Reggie Young
  d. Mike Utley

Q40. What song on the *A1A* album alludes to this incident?
   a. "Presents to Send You"
   b. "Life is Just a Tire Swing"
   c. "Migration"
   d. "Tin Cup Chalice"

THE ANSWERS

A1. For licensing reasons, I won't reprint the entire verse and chorus of "Why Don't We Get Drunk," but if you were able to sing your way through to the title line, take 5 points.

A2. c

A3. Actually, all of them did, so give yourself 1 point for each name that you picked. The United Artists film, which featured a soundtrack by Buffett, is based on the misadventures of a pair of cattle rustlers. The movie was critically well received but, unfortunately, the soundtrack didn't sell well. It went out of print, making it a much sought after collector's item among Buffett fans.

A4. a is right, so take 5 points if you said so. In case you missed it, b is the name of a Roy Rogers hamburger.

A5. b. That's the author, Tom McGuane, playing mandolin with Jimmy.

A6. There were Marvin Gardens (also credited as the songwriter for the saucy "Why Don't We Get Drunk and Screw"), Miss Kay Pasa, Miss Kitty Litter, and Al Vacado.

A7. a. No, but Jerry Jeff did cowrite one song on the album with JB.

b. Yes (5 points). McGuane, besides being a close friend and the author of the best-selling novel, *Ninety-Two in the Shade*, would also eventually become Buffett's brother-in-law.

c. No—a silly choice, really, since Marty Robbins is the man who had the original hit of a song titled "A White Sport Coat and a Pink Carnation" (no. 2 in April 1957).

    d. Well, take 2 points, because he does take space to thank "Bob Hall and the Thompson O'Neal Shrimp Co. for supplying the pink crustaceans which made a great cover and a fine dinner."

A8. b

A9. c

A10. b. "Ballad of Spider John" and "God's Own Drunk" are the only songs credited to someone else. That's worth 5 points. If you picked c, I'll give you partial credit, since "Brand New Country Star" was cowritten with J. Arnold (you can have 2 points for being close).

A11. c. The only song in ¾ time on the entire record is "West Nashville Grand Ballroom Gown," making the relevance of the album's title somewhat vague. For those of you who answered d, I'm not gonna give you partial credit this time, but I will quickly explain what ¾ time is. In musical parlance, ¾ is a time signature signifying 3 quarter-note beats to a measure. A typical example of ¾ time would be anything that is described as a waltz (**1**,2,3,**1**,2,3).

A12. b. "Door Number Three" was written by Steve Goodman *and* Jimmy Buffett, so that doesn't count.

A13. c ("I've got my Hush Puppies on..."). By the way, this lyrical phrase caused some problems in England, where the song was refused airplay on the government-run BBC since it was viewed as a free endorsement for a product. He allegedly rerecorded the line for overseas release, singing "hiking boots" in place of "Hush Puppies" to appease the English censors, but another "artist" beat him to it! Jonathan King, the pop artist/parodist best known for "Everyone's Gone to the Moon," released his own version, singing about "tennis shoes."

A14. b. Unbelievable, I know, but it's Johnny Mathis who croons the theme song to this ultraviolent film.

A15. c. Ex-football player Joe Don Baker played Pusser in the first *Walking Tall* movie. Bo Svenson replaced Baker for *Walking Tall, Part Two* and *Walking Tall—The Final*

Chapter. Incidentally, Pusser himself was slated for the role (!), but was killed in a car accident before filming began.

A16. c. "The Great Filling Station Hold Up" b/w "They Don't Dance Like Carmen No More" was the first single pressed. It didn't reach the national pop charts, but it did go to no. 58 on the Country charts. A second single was later pressed with "Why Don't We Get Drunk" on the B-side, intended for jukebox release only.

A17. The album is *A1A* (I figured we'd get the novices to guess the more obvious *Living and Dying in ¾ Time* album) and the song is "Nautical Wheelers." Take 2 points for the right album title, and 3 points if you guessed the correct song.

A18. d. Six of his seven self-penned songs mention drink in some fashion. Want me to prove it? OK—1) "Presents to Send You"—"There sits a fifth of tequila," 2) "A Pirate Looks at Forty"— "I have been drunk now for over two weeks," 3) "Migration"—"pull the cork out of a bottle of wine," 4) "Trying to Reason with Hurricane Season"—"I knew I could use a bloody mary," 5) "Nautical Wheelers"—"shuffle on down to the bar" and finally, 6) "Tin Cup Chalice"—"Gimme oysters and beer for dinner every day of the year." The lone exception is "Life is Just a Tire Swing."

By the way, three of these six songs also mention drugs: 1) "Presents to Send You"—"My plans took a skid when I smoked the whole lid" (for those of you who didn't live through the seventies, "lid" is a slang term for an ounce of marijuana), 2) "A Pirate Looks at Forty"—"I've run my share of grass," and 3) "Tin Cup Chalice"—"get high by the sea there."

A19. c

A20. b-2. For Northerners like me who aren't familiar with the Krystal's chain, they're a fairly ubiquitous presence all over Tennessee, selling hamburgers on the cheap twenty-four hours a day.

A21. d. Before his partner jumps out with a pellet gun, he politely asks for "fifty cents worth, please."

A22. "…just a little bit shady."

A23. "…bathing suit, chew a little Juicy Fruit, wash away the night."

A24. "I'd like to ride the rodeo but I've got…"

A25. Kim and Jim

A26. c

A27. d. He also married an actress namd Kim.

A28. a

A29. 4-a, 4-b, 4-c, 3-d. The first three are the participants of the doomed love triangle in "Cuban Crime of Passion." "Ricky" is the guy whose job it was to watch the security mirror during the "Peanut Butter Conspiracy."

A30. Carmen Miranda and Xavier Cougat. Back in the days before the United States imposed an embargo on Fidel Castro's Cuba, the large island to the immediate south of Florida was making quite a cultural impression on its neighbor to the north. Before the Cuban Missile Crisis essentially destroyed all interaction between Cuba and the United States, Carmen Miranda was wowing Americans with her fanciful act of singing and dancing, most memorably with a basket of fruit on her head. Many people remember her as the focal point of an advertising campaign for Chiquita bananas. Xavier Cougat was a famous and extraordinarily talented bandleader. Typically, though, most Americans remember him instead as the aged husband of Charo, the "hoochie-coochie" girl.

A31. According to the lyrics of "I Have Found Me a Home," "My old red bike gets me around to the bars and beaches of my town."

A32. "My Lovely Lady." "She," by the way, is none other than Jimmy's future wife, Jane Slogsvol.

A33. "Death of an Unpopular Poet"

A34. "Come Monday"

A35. "Livingston Saturday Night." I know what you're thinking... "Wait a minute, that line isn't on the album," right?
Well, you're right, but it *did* appear this way on the movie
soundtrack. Since it's been out of print for years, I would
suppose that you are only familiar with the version that
appears on *Son of a Son of a Sailor*. For that version,
Buffett softened a few of the more "blue" phrases that
appeared on the original soundtrack version and this line
is one of those that was edited.

A36. 1) Boston Blackie, 2) Ricky Ricardo, 3) Andy Devine, 4)
Sky's niece, Penny, 5) Rama of the Jungle, and 6) the Sheik
of Araby. Take 1 point if you could only name one, 2 points
for two, and 5 points if you could name at least three.

A37. 1) "Ridin' in Style," 2) "Cattle Truckin,'" 3) The Wrangler,"
4) "Some Gothic Ranch Action," 5) "15 Gears," and 6)
"Rancho Deluxe-Instrumental" (Duh). Score the same as
above (1 point for one, 2 points for two, and 3 points for at
least three).

A38. d

A39. a

A40. a. In "Presents to Send You," Buffett sings "I had my hair
pulled out by a man who really wasn't my friend."

Score Results

I assume by now that you have gotten into the swing of things
and are having a good time. If you've gotten this far, then you
are either satisfied to be learning as you go, or are anxious to
see if you're as smart as you think. This test covered a classic
period from Buffett's career, but fans who are new to Jimmy
might have struggled a bit here. Your score will determine if
your knowledge is up to snuff, or if you need to buy a few
records from this time period.

0–50 points—Let's see if we can invent a good excuse for you…you just got into Buffett recently, and haven't had time to catch up on the old stuff yet…yeah, that's it! Well, rather than continuing to take pot shots in the dark, you ought to check out at least some of the albums that are covered in this chapter (and the next). Then, try taking the test again (we'll let it slide this time).

51–100 points—Maybe you're like the person above, but you've had a bit more time to listen to Buffett's older work. Well, now you know that you need to know more, especially if you want to play with the big boys and girls (those crazies at the concerts with the insane clothing). You already like the guy, right? So then, buying a few albums from his classic early years will certainly do you no harm. They're not too expensive, and for consistency are some of the most reliable Buffett recordings you can buy. It might even make you a fan for life.

101–150 points—You're a fan, all right, but your obsession is tempered by reason. Or then again, maybe common sense has nothing to do with it at all. Maybe you're the type of person who once traded his monthly meal ticket for a seat with a restricted view in the 287th row. Maybe you're so blindly obsessed with the Parrot Head phenomenon that you don't even bother yourself with the minutiae of Buffett's career. Maybe the only thing that matters to you is having a good time. You're willing to go hungry for a month, because the experience will be worth it. Now, that is a fan. Crazy? Absolutely, but still a fan.

151–200 points—Either you're over thirty-five and have been a fan since the early days, or you are one serious Parrot Head. Even as you read this, you are probably scoffing at the very notion of a Buffett quiz that is designed to trip you up. Well, don't get too cocky, because there are five more chapters, and then there's the ultra-tough Final Trivia Quiz. I still might get you, but for now, congratulations and well done.

3

The Late Seventies

The late seventies were marked by a significant increase in Jimmy Buffett's national exposure. Although his first top 40 single, "Come Monday," afforded him a reasonable amount of attention, it would have been impossible for anybody to predict the phenomenal career that would be spawned by his first and only top 10 hit, "Margaritaville." Thanks mostly to the overwhelming reaction to this song during the summer of 1977, Jimmy Buffett was transformed from a somewhat obscure singer-songwriter with a following that was increasing slowly but steadily to a household name on the verge of superstardom.

Along with his increased recognition came new management, new record producers, a new sailboat, a new home, a new marriage and most importantly (from a musical perspective), a new band. Gone were the fictitious Coral Reefers, replaced by an authentic band that not only understood Buffett's unique stylings but would also go out on the road with him. Due to the influx of corporate mergers and high-finance buyouts that set in during the latter half of the seventies, he would also find himself with a new record label before the decade ended. For the most part, though, his approach to songwriting remained pretty much the same. The Gulf-Western formula he had perfected in the early '70s would continue to serve him well, but the now "official" Coral Reefer Band would add some muscle to his ideas, giving his output a bit more of a rock flavor while slowly moving him away from the Nashville-based sound of his earlier records. As an appropriate symbol of the times and also of his stardom, Jimmy Buffett became the subject of a feature article in *Rolling Stone* magazine's October 4, 1979, issue. For a man who managed to keep his ambitions in check (or at least out of plain sight) Jimmy Buffett ended the seventies sitting on top of the world and was preparing to climb even higher.

Since this stage marks one of Buffett's most popular phases, chances are fairly good that you are familiar with much of his work during these years. For that reason, I have gone out of my way to ensure that this particular group of questions is tougher than previous sections. A reasonably in-depth knowledge of Buffett ephemera will be very useful to you in this section. Albums that are covered in this quiz include

Havana Daydreamin	1976
Changes in Latitudes, Changes in Attitudes	1977
Son of a Son of a Sailor	1978
You Had to Be There	1978
Volcano	1979

QUIZ

Complete the following lyrical phrases:

Q1. "Don't try to describe the ocean (or 'the scenery,' or 'a Kiss Concert') if you've never seen it…"

Q2. "With all of our running and all of our cunning…"

Q3. "She had a ballpark figure…"

Q4. "Lava come down soft and hot…"

Provide answers to the following:

Q5. What's the name of the shop where Jimmy was going to buy chocolate milk to help cure his hangover?

Q6. What was the original "working title" for the album *Havana Daydreamin'*?

Q7. Which Jimmy Buffett song mentions pop singer, religious right figurehead, outspoken advocate of intolerance, and orange juice pusher Anita Bryant by name?

Q8. In 1979, Buffett made his second on-screen appearance, performing one of his songs. Name the movie (2 points), then name the song (3 points).

Q9. What was Jimmy nibbling on while waiting for his shrimp to boil?

Q10. What is the significance of the gold anchor that can be seen hanging from Jimmy's neck on the cover of *You Had to Be There?*

Q11. On the studio version of "Landfall," Buffett sings "What would I do if I met Lucille Ball?" Which celebrity does he invoke on the *You Had to Be There* album?

Q12. Before "Changes in Latitudes, Changes in Attitudes" was released as a single, one of the lines was altered. "Good times and riches and son of a bitches" was revised so as to not be offensive or hurt the song's chances of airplay. What was the revised line?

Back to multiple choice...

Q13. Which two of the following songs did Buffett share writing credit with his soon-to-be wife, Jane Slogsvol? (2 points for one, 5 points for both)
   a. "Tampico Trauma"
   b. "Kick It in Second Wind"
   c. "Something So Feminine About a Mandolin"
   d. "Cliches"
   e. "Presents to Send You"

Q14. Where was *Havana Daydreamin'* recorded?
   a. Florida
   b. Alabama
   c. Tennessee
   d. Texas
   e. California

Q15. Who sings back-up on "My Head Hurts, My Feet Stink, and I Don't Love Jesus"?
    a. The Oak Ridge Boys
    b. Alabama
    c. The Statler Brothers
    d. The Lennon Sisters

Q16. In late 1976, a Jimmy Buffett interview appeared in the pages of *High Times*, a magazine that openly celebrated the widespread drug culture of the times. Who appeared on the cover of that issue?
    a. A caricature of Richard Nixon and Spiro Agnew
    b. Jimmy Buffett
    c. Santa Claus
    d. Mona Lisa

Q17. On the inner sleeve of *Changes in Latitudes, Changes in Attitudes*, which of the following pen sketches accompany the lyrics to "Margaritaville" (pick as few or as many as you think are correct)?
    a. A salt shaker
    b. A bald guy in a bathing suit standing by a road sign
    c. A bottle of tequila
    d. A record
    e. A forearm with a "girly" tattoo
    f. A paunchy guy reclining in a hammock
    g. A steaming pot of boiling shrimp

Q18. What was one of the more popular nicknames of Jimmy's manager, Irving Azoff?
    a. Cuddles
    b. Huggsy-Wuggsy
    c. Bambi
    d. The Poison Dwarf

Q19. On the poster provided with the *You Had to Be There* album, Jimmy is clearly seen wearing a custom-made T-shirt. What does the shirt say?
    a. You Had to Be There
    b. Camellia Grill, New Orleans

    c. Where in the HELL is Irving?

    d. Patience my ass, I'm going to kill someone

Q20. Which of the following novels does Jimmy quote from on the inner sleeve of *Son of a Son of a Sailor?*

    a. *Wind From the Carolinas,* by Robert Wilder

    b. *The Adventures of Tom Sawyer,* by Mark Twain

    c. *The Sound and the Fury,* by William Faulkner

    d. *Don't Stop the Carnival,* by Herman Wouk

    e. *To Have and Have Not,* by Ernest Hemingway

Q21. Judging by the fact that you're taking this quiz, I'd say it's a safe bet that you've heard the song "Margaritaville" until it was coming out of your ears. Well, then, let's see how well you were listening. In concert, Buffett often includes a fourth verse that was excised from the original release. If you've been paying attention at the concerts, or listening closely enough to the *You Had to Be There* live album, I figure that you should be able to rattle off this extra verse without hesitation. Go for it.

Q22. Here's something that might interest you: Can you guess which of the following songs was at no. 1 while "Margaritaville" was peaking at is highest chart spot of no. 8?
   a. "Looks Like We Made It"—Barry Manilow
   b. "Da Doo Ron Ron"—Shaun Cassidy
   c. "I Just Wanna Be Your Everything"—Andy Gibb
   d. "Gonna Fly Now" (Theme from *Rocky*)—Bill Conti
   e. "Undercover Angel"—Alan O'Day

Q23. While on tour with this band, Buffett leased his apartment to a famous (or perhaps "infamous" is more appropriate) tenant. Who?
   a. Warren Beatty
   b. Harrison Ford
   c. Don Henley
   d. Hunter Thompson

Q24. What album did the usually positive-leaning *Record World* magazine review by stating that it "had something to offend everyone"?
   a. "Volcano"
   b. "You Had to Be There"
   c. "Son of a Son of a Sailor"
   d. "Havana Daydreamin'"

Q25. Which of the following songs from *Changes in Latitudes, Changes in Attitudes* are written by Jimmy Buffett?
   a. "Lovely Cruise"
   b. "Banana Republics"
   c. "Biloxi"
   d. "Tampico Trauma"

Q26. The movie *FM* was yet another film to feature a version of "Livingston Saturday Night" (*Rancho Deluxe* was the first). Which one of the following artists did *not* also appear on this movie's soundtrack album?
   a. Billy Joel
   b. Poco

c. Bob Seger

d. The Eagles

The end of multiple choice. For the next few questions, you'll once again need to supply the answer yourself.

Q27. After the royalties began rolling in from "Come Monday" and subsequent albums, Jimmy treated himself a thirty-three foot Cheoy Lee ketch. What did he name the boat?

Q28. Now, I could be especially cruel and ask you for the exact date of the Buffett wedding, but I won't do that—the date was August 27. Now, you tell me the year of this event.

Q29. Later that same year, Jimmy's sister would also get married. To whom?

Q30. 1975 marked the first year that Jimmy Buffett had a real honest-to-goodness touring band, one that would also follow him into the studio for the *Havana Daydreamin'* sessions. Fingers Taylor was a member, while Mike Utley, at this time, was not. Can you name the guitarist, bass player, *and* drummer from this historic lineup?

Q31. In "Life Is Just a Tire Swing," what is it that Jimmy remembers smelling whenever he visited his "crazy old uncle and aunt"?

a. Jasmine

b. Honeysuckle vine

c. Magnolias

d. The creosote plant

e. Bougainvillea

Q32. In the same lyrics, what song did Jimmy claim was the only song he could sing?

Q33. In "Door Number Three," what is the singer's costume?

Q34. Name the song that contains the following couplet:
"I know the night and I miss it
I've got this thing for applause."

a. "Perrier Blues"

b. "Miss You So Badly"

    c. "Stranded on a Sandbar"
    d. "Dreamsicle"

Q35. In "Trying to Reason With Hurricane Season," what does Jimmy estimate the windspeed to be when he decides to close the shutters?
    a. "Over forty miles an hour"
    b. "Gusting to seventy knots"
    c. "Fifty knots or thereabouts"
    d. "It felt like it was blowing sixty"

Q36. Which of the following does Jimmy use to help cure his hangover in "My Head Hurts, My Feet Stink, and I Don't Love Jesus"?
    a. Darvon
    b. Chocolate milk
    c. Orange juice
    d. Aspirin

Q37. In the song "This Hotel Room," I count at least twenty acoutrements that are accounted for in the lyrics. Name at least ten of them and take a point for each correct pair you can come up with. Only exact matches count.

Q38. Here's a strange one: I have the temerity to insist that the lyric sheet included with the *Son of a Son of a Sailor* album (printed on the album's inner sleeve) has a glaring misprint in the song "Manana." The line reads "Don't ever forget that you just may wind up being *gone.*" Assuming that you will agree with me on this, what does Jimmy actually say?

Q39. On *You Had to Be There*, what movie does Jimmy plug before launching into "Wonder Why We Ever Go Home"?
    a. *FM*
    b. *Rancho Deluxe*
    c. *Animal House*
    d. *National Lampoon's Vacation*

Q40. Name at least five of the ten places where Jimmy does *not* want to land after the volcano blows (one point for each).

ANSWERS

A1. "...Don't ever forget that you just may wind up being wrong" (or "in my song," or "being gonged"—remember *The Gong Show*?) (3 points for *any* of the above) from "Manana" (2 points)

A2. "...If we couldn't laugh, we would all go insane." (3 points), from "Changes in Latitudes, Changes in Attitudes" (2 points). By the way, you should have had this *exact* phrase, since the alternate lyric choices are preceded by a slightly different phrase ("my" instead of "our," for example).

A3. "...he had a ballpoint pen." (3 points), from "Cliches" (2 points)

A4. "...You better lava me now or lava me not" (3 points), from "Volcano" (2 points)

A5. Fausto's

A6. *Second Wind*. Apparently, an album with this title came very close to release, since acetates are rumored to exist. This version of the album included three song titles that were deleted from the final product—"Please Take Your Drunken Fifteen-Year-Old Girlfriend Home," "Train to Dixieland," and "Wonder Why You Ever Go Home" (from *Rancho Deluxe* and to appear later on *Changes in Latitudes, Changes in Attitudes*).

A7. In "Manana," Jimmy declares that "I hope Anita Bryant never does one of my songs." As of yet, it hasn't happened, either.

A8. *FM*. With a title song by Steely Dan, *FM* was meant to convey life at an alternative FM radio station. Unfortunately, the movie's release came after the onset of punk rock, and its subject matter seemed more than a little dated and wrongheaded at the time of release. The song performed by Buffett in the film was "Livingston Saturday Night," marking its second appearance in as many films.

A9.   Sponge cake (5 points) ("Nibblin' on sponge cake, watching the sun bake all of those tourists...")

A10. He wears this anchor in lieu of a wedding ring.

A11. Lauren Bacall

A12. "Good times and riches, some bruises and stitches" (5 points if you knew this). Besides the lyric change, the song was also remixed with a pronounced emphasis on the syrupy string arrangement.

A13. b and c. Both of the songs that were cocredited to Jane appear back to back on the second side of the *Havana Daydreamin'* album.

A14. c. *Tracks for Havana Daydreamin'* were recorded and mixed at two different studios, both in the suburbs just outside of Nashville. Youngun Sound is in Murfreesboro and the Creative Workshop is in Berry Hill, both in Tennessee. Jimmy had been recording off and on at the Creative Workshop ever since his Barnaby days. Many fans don't realize it, but virtually every one of Jimmy's recording sessions up to this point had taken place in or around Nashville. Not until *Changes in Latitudes, Changes in Attitudes* would he release an album that was (mostly) recorded elsewhere.

A15. a

A16. c

A17. a through d are correct. Take 1 point for each correct answer and deduct 1 point for each wrong answer. Take 5 points if you guessed all four correctly.
      The road sign reads "Margaritaville 4 or 5 miles," while an arrow points to the record, saying, "OLD CHAMPS RECORD," referring to the band that recorded the early '60s instrumental "Tequila."

A18. d

A19. c

A20. a. "There had been a time when the settlement had made a profitable living from the wrecking of ships, either through the changing of lights or connivance with an unscrupulous captain....Then there would be a time of riotous living with most of the community drunk and wandering about in an aimless daze until the purchased rum was gone. After that the residents sat moodily in the sun and waited for something to happen."

I believe this to be a reference to the native "conchs" of Key West around the turn of the century.

A21. "Old Men in tank tops cruisin' the gift shops
Checkin' out chiquitas down by the shore
They think about weight loss,
wish they could be their own boss,
Those three-day vacations become quite a bore."

A22. a. "Margaritaville" peaked at no. 8 for the week of 7/23/77 while Barry Manilow's "Looks Like We Made It" sat at the top of the charts. As much as it pains me to report this, all of the songs listed as choices for this question are actual no. 1 hits from the month of July 1977—bad movie themes, shmaltzy bubble-gum pop, and cheesy disco, sometimes sung by the kid brothers of teen idols. Yeesh, what a summer. Taking this into consideration, it's no wonder that "Margaritaville" made such an impact.

A23. d

A24. d

A25. Only d. Any other choice yields no points, even if you picked d in tandem with another selection. For your information, "Lovely Cruise" was written by Jonathan Banam, "Banana Republics" by Steve Goodman, and "Biloxi" by Jesse Winchester.

A26. b

A27. *Euphoria*

A28. 1977

A29. Novelist Tom McGuane, the author of *Rancho Deluxe* and *92 in the Shade*, among others

A30. The guitarist was Roger Bartlett, the bassist was Harry Dailey, and the drummer was Phillip Fajardo. Take a point for each name you came up with, or 5 points if you could name all three.

A31. d

A32. "Jambalaya" (by Hank Williams, by the way)

A33. a beer barrel ("I chose my apparel, I wore a beer barrel…")

A34. a (from the *You Had to Be There* album)

A35. c

A36. a, b, and c. No aspirin, though. Take a point for each correct choice (subtract a point if you chose aspirin) and give yourself 5 points if you chose a, b, and c only.

A37. A laundry bag, a shoe-shine cloth, thirty-two hangers, a touch-tone phone, a light that comes on, an air conditioner, a radiator, two big chairs, a holy bible, a *TV Guide*, a sign that reads "do not disturb," a monogrammed towel, a bucket of ice, a chest of drawers, a mirror that lies, a room service menu, a porcelain throne, an aluminum sink, two big pillows, "magic fingers," and a king-size bed. Whew—remember, there's a 5 point maximum on each question.

A38. He says "gonged," not gone. The line is a reference to the goofy late-seventies daytime TV (non) talent contest called *The Gong Show*, where celebrities would rate the questionable talents of the show's guests. FYI, Buffett mentions this show outright in the lyrics to the song "Miss You So Badly." (Judging from his lyrics, somebody was watching an awful lot of television, wouldn't you say?)

A39. c

A40. 1) New York City, 2) Mexico, 3) Three Mile Island, 4) Commanche Sky Park, 5) Nashville, Tennessee, 6) San Juan Airport, 7) Yukon territory, 8) San Diego, 9) Buzzard's Bay, and finally, 10) on the Ayatollah.

Score Time

0–50 points—I *told* you it was going to get harder. If you want to continue, my advice is that you stop now and collect your bearings (i.e., listen to the music). If this was an SAT test, you would have been sent home by now.

51–100 points—Eh. You did better on the earlier sections, didn't you? I tried to warn you, but nnoooo-oooo, you wouldn't listen. Don't feel too bad, but I'd brush up if I were you.

101–150 points—Not bad, not bad. This is one of Buffett's most popular phases but a few of the questions here were undeniably tough. Can you hang on for the upcoming chapters?

151–200 points—I'm impressed! Not only did I decrease your chances of survival by lessening the multiple choice questions, but the questions themselves were tougher here, too. If you did well here, then you might be a tougher nut to crack than I had expected.

4

The Early Eighties

Few things can be as fickle as the pop music industry, and just a few years after "Margaritaville" left a permanent impression on the American audience, the music scene began to shift in a new direction. The main reason for Buffett's decline in popularity had more to do with changing musical tastes than with any decrease in the quality of his output, but punk and new wave trends were essentially foreign to Buffett. Rather than force himself to adapt to the revised tastes of a constantly changing audience, he opted to remain true to himself musically, while coming up with a few new and interesting ideas that just might help him to hang on.

Now that he had a family, his personal time was more precious than ever and Buffet worked hard to maintain a balance between his two principal obligations. Another factor that competed for attention was his dedication to various causes, most notably his "Save the Manatee" organization. Also, it was around this time that Buffett's desire to write developed into something more than whimsy and he set out to complete his first collection of short stories and a movie script based on his time in Key West, which he called *Evening in Mar-*

garitaville. With so many things demanding Buffett's attention, the Coral Reefer Band was temporarily waylaid.

His manager, Irving Azoff, was a key player in contributing Buffett's material to soundtracks and he continued as such, with songs being featured in *Urban Cowboy* and *Fast Times at Ridgemont High*. After a fierce legal battle, Irving Azoff found himself at the helm of MCA Records, putting Buffett in the unique and somewhat awkward position of having both his management and his record label answering to the same person. With popular music now squarely in the hands of new-wavers, though, Buffett's future looked somewhat less than secure. To alleviate the stylistic differences, he avoided main-stream pop and focused much of his attention on Nashville. By consciously re-embracing the Gulf-Western style that he had started with, he hoped that he could maintain at least a segment of his former popularity. Meanwhile, he also began to set the wheels in motion for a number of projects that just might have the potential of rebuilding his previous constituency. The albums that were released for this phase of his career are:

Coconut Telegraph	1981
Somewhere Over China	1982
One Particular Harbor	1983
Riddles in the Sand	1984

THE QUIZ

Q1. What hit album from the 1980s featured a version of Buffett's "Changes in Latitudes, Changes in Attitudes"?
   a. *The Wrestling Album*
   b. *The Great Muppet Caper*
   c. *The "Miami Vice" Soundtrack*
   d. *Jane Fonda's Workout Record*
   e. *Changes in Latitudes, Changes in Attitudes*
   f. *You Had to Be There*

Q2. What song did Jimmy Buffett record for the *Urban Cowboy* soundtrack?
   a. "Hey There, Mr. Cowboy Man"
   b. "Sailin' to Texas"
   c. "Saturday Night Fightin' Fever"
   d. "Hello Texas"

Q3. Who designed the graphics for *Coconut Telegraph?*
   a. Walter Hunt
   b. George Seurat
   c. Paul Signac
   d. Charles Angrand

Q4. What country-based "outlaw" artist began to appear on the scene about this time, whom numerous critics tended to compare unfavorably to Buffett?
   a. Waylon Jennings
   b. Tompall Glaser
   c. David Allen Coe
   d. Will Jennings

Q5. On the album cover for *Somewhere Over China,* on what continent are Jimmy's feet firmly planted?
   a. China, duh
   b. Europe (one foot Western, one foot Eastern)
   c. North America
   d. South America
   e. Africa

Q6. Which of the following songs were cowritten with Dave Loggins?
   a. "Island"
   b. "The Good Fight"
   c. "Treat Her Like a Lady"
   d. "Stars on the Water"

Q7. "Stars Fell on Alabama," a song Jimmy covered on the *Coconut Telegraph* album, was written by Mitchell Parish and Frank Perkins. Which of the following artists had previously recorded their own versions of the tune?
   a. Frankie Laine
   b. Georgia Gibbs

c. Don Cornell

d. Guy Lombardo

e. Richard Himber

Q8. Since we're discussing real oldies, let me tell you a few things about the author of "Slow Boat to China." Frank Loesser had a reputation for his excessive smoking and his fiery temper. He died of emphysema at seventy-nine with a pack of cigarettes next to the bed, but in his prime, his songwriting prowess was regarded with awe. Other songs he was known for that you may recognize include "Praise the Lord and Pass the Amunition," "Baby It's Cold Outside," the entire score to *Guys and Dolls* ("Luck Be a Lady," "A Bushel and a Peck," etc.), the *Hans Christian Anderson* soundtrack—a childhood favorite of mine—including "Thumbelina," "Inchworm," and "Wonderful Copenhagen," (he received an Oscar nomination for this one) as well as the score to *How to Succeed in Business Without Really Trying*. This earned him a Pulitzer prize. Now, then, since we're getting so historic, I figured you'd like to guess which of the following artists preceded Jimmy Buffet with their own recordings of "Slow Boat to China."

a. Kay Kaiser

b. Freddie Martin

c. Eddy Howard

d. Benny Goodman

e. Francis Albert Sinatra

Q9. For which of the following television soap operas did Buffett do a very quick cameo walk-on appearance?

a. *As the World Turns*

b. *Days of Our Lives*

c. *All My Children*

d. *Guiding Light*

Q10. While we're on the subject, what was the name of Buffett's character in that soap opera?

a. Haystacks Calhoun

b. Randy Clyde

    c. Jimmy Buffet (with one *t*), a "caterer and lounge singer extraordinaire"

    d. Chainsaw McGregor

Q11. Billy Clyde was a character from Liz Ashley's soap who was constantly finagling a scam that would net him enough money to retire somewhere in the Caribbean. What Buffett song mentions this less than palatable character?

    a. "We Are the People Our Parents Warned Us About"

    b. "It's Midnight and I'm Not Famous Yet"

    c. "Weather is Here, Wish You Were Beautiful"

    d. "I Wish Lunch Could Last Forever"

Q12. The Key West Rebellion against the Reagan administration's war on drugs led them to declare their independence from the United States. What name did the Key West rebels apply to their fictionally independent state?

    a. Fredonia

    b. Margaritaville

    c. The Conch Republic

    d. Yoknapatawpha

Q13. There are a pair of gambling terms that are used in the lyrics to "It's Midnight and I'm Not Famous Yet." One is a "thirty-two hop" and the other is a ten dollar "yo." I'm feeling generous, so you only have to define one of these, but accurately, for full credit.

Q14. Since we're off of multiple choice, try this. The following quote appears on the back cover of the *Somewhere Over China* album—"It's young people who put life into ritual by making conventions a living part of life. Only old people destroy life by making it a ritual. The boy that belongs to a secret pirate's gang and who dreams of defending an abstraction with his blood hasn't quite died out before twenty-one, you know." Without looking, tell me who wrote it (3 points), and the name of the work that it was extracted from (2 points).

Q15. The inner sleeve of the *One Particular Harbor* album features a photo of Buffett holding something up to his ear. What is it?
   a. A coconut
   b. A boombox
   c. A conch shell
   d. A compact disc

Q16. In 1985, Mike Nesmith released a ninety-minute collection of comedy and music. This film featured a Buffett video for which song?
   a. "One Particular Harbor"
   b. "Coconut Telegraph"
   c. "La Vie Dansante"
   d. "Last Mango In Paris"

Q17. Which of the following songs were *not* cowritten with (or written exclusively by) Steve Goodman?
   a. "It's Midnight and I'm Not Famous Yet"
   b. "Where's the Party"
   c. "Incommunicado"
   d. "California Promises"

Q18. Which of the following songs were *not* cowritten with Michael Utley?
   a. "When the Wild Life Betrays Me"
   b. "Livin' It Up"
   c. "I Heard I Was in Town"
   d. "I Used to Have Money One Time"

Finish the following two lyric phrases:

Q19. "Seldom found the trick to arithmetic, three plus two be..."

Q20. "Crack went my leg like the shell of an egg..."

Q21. During the winter tour of 1979–80, a member of Buffett's entourage slipped on ice and broke his collarbone. Who?
   a. Mike Utley   c. Josh Leo
   b. Fingers Taylor   d. Barry Chance

Q22. Buffett bought a smaller custom-built twenty-six foot
sailboat to replace the much larger Cheoy Lee that he had
been using. What did he name this boat?
   a. *Euphoria*
   b. *Euphoria II*
   c. *Savannah Jane*
   d. *Lady of the Waters*

Q23. Which song from the *Coconut Telegraph* album was
chosen as the representative single?
   a. "Growing Older But Not Up"
   b. "Weather is Here, Wish You Were Beautiful"
   c. "It's My Job"
   d. "Coconut Telegraph"

Q24. In 1982, Buffett was one of a handful of artists chosen to
sing for a beer company, prompting Buffett to say, "This is

the closest thing I've had to an AM hit in years." What product was Buffett singing about?

   a. Miller

   b. Budweiser

   c. Heineken

   d. Corona

Q25. What was the original working title for the sessions that would eventually become the *One Particular Harbor* album?

   a. *Train to Dixie*

   b. *Second Wind*

   c. *Twelve Volt Man*

   d. *The Dog Ate My Homework and Other Great Excuses*

Q26. As mentioned earlier, Buffett contributed a video in 1983 to a Michael Nesmith video/comedy compilation. What was the name of the project?

   a. *Elephant Parts*

   b. *Doctor Duck's Super Secret All-Purpose Sauce*

   c. *Repo Man*

   d. *Monkee See, Monkee Do*

Q27. After the upheaval that took place at MCA, resulting in Irving Azoff's placement at the company's helm, a new producer was assigned to Buffett. Who was it?

   a. Norbert Putnam

   b. Jimmy Bowen

   c. Buzz Cason

   d. Russ Kunkel

   e. Michael Utley

Q28. According to the song's lyrics, on what day does the "Coconut Telegraph" take a rest or, in other words, what day is it when the lines have all gone dead?

   a. Sunday

   b. Friday

   c. Wednesday

   d. Thursday

Q29. What song mentions the movies *Red River* and *Liberty Valence?*
  a. "The Good Fight"
  b. Somewhere Over China"
  c. "Incommunicado"
  d. "If I Could Just Get It on Paper"

Q30. What is the occupation of the optimistic laborer in "It's My Job"?
  a. Truck driver
  b. Street sweeper
  c. Street musician
  d. Banker

Q31. Match the real-life character with the song that refers to him.

a. Pete Rose	1. "Somewhere Over China"
b. John Wayne	2. "Incommunicado"
c. Marco Polo	3. "I'm Growing Older But Not
d. Gardner McKay	Up"
e. Robin Leach	4. "We Are the People Our Parents Warned Us About"
	5. "King of Somewhere Hot"

Q32. The gatefold inner sleeve for the *Coconut Telegraph* album features a full-sized drawing that combines an electronic device and a fruit. What is the combination?
  a. Banana/telephone
  b. Coconut/headphones
  c. Mango/radio
  d. Watermelon/boombox

Q33. Which of the below song titles features the actions of a character named Lester Polyester?
  a. "The Weather Is Here, Wish You Were Beautiful"
  b. "Who's the Blond Stranger"
  c. "It's Midnight and I'm Not Famous Yet"
  d. "Somewhere Over China"

Q34. What song mentions Buffett's desire to fly the space shuttle?
  a. "Come to the Moon"
  b. "Stars Fell on Alabama"
  c. "It's Midnight and I'm Not Famous Yet"
  d. "Somewhere Over China"

Q35. To be honest, I don't get this dedication at all, so why not ask the question and see if it makes more sense to you than it does to me: What song from *Somewhere Over China* is introduced in the liner notes with "For anyone who loves Creole Cookin' and New Orleans music"?
  a. "Where's the Party"
  b. "Stars on the Water"
  c. "Lip Service"
  d. "Creola"

Q36. Another album's comments has the following dedication: "To Muhammed Ali for twenty years of excitement and entertainment." Name the song that was dedicated to the man who could float like a butterfly and sting like a bee. (Okay, I'll give you the album title: it's *One Particular Harbor*.)

Q37. According to the lyrics of "Honey Do," what two letters cannot be pronounced when speaking "Southern-ese"?

Q38. What Buffett song features a short snippet of the Isley Brothers' (or the Beatles') song "Twist and Shout"?
  a. "We Are the People Our Parents Warned Us About"
  b. "Livin' It Up"
  c. "La Vie Dansante"
  d. "Slow Boat to China"

Q39. Why is "this Joe in Mexico" called the "Twelve Volt Man"?
  a. Because he operates a generator-powered blender and radio
  b. Because he once got electrocuted while singing into a microphone that was too close to the beach
  c. Because he lives off of solar power
  d. Because he's the only licensed electrician in town

Q40. Three of the following four people are credited for singing background vocals on "I Used to Have Money One Time." Pick them.
   a. Bonnie Bramlett
   b. Rita Coolidge
   c. Frank Bama
   d. Timothy B. Schmit

THE ANSWERS

A1. d. Listed by Joel Whitburn's *Billboard Books* as an aerobics album, it entered the album charts in May 1982 and climbed all the way to no. 15. It remained on the charts for 120 weeks! Other "feature" artists included Boz Scaggs ("Harbor Lights"), REO Speedwagon ("In Your Letter"), and the Jacksons ("Can You Feel It?"). While Buffett sings away in the background, Fonda can be heard imploring "Ready for buttocks tucks?" "Squeeze it! Squeeze it!" The song does also appear on d and e, but these albums were released in the '70s.

A2. d. The song was not written by Buffett but by Brian Collins and Robby Campbell

A3. a. The album's style can be traced to the work of French Impressionist Georges Seurat (b), who is often recognized as the founder of the arduous style known as pointillism. One of the best-known examples of this style is Seurat's "A Sunday Afternoon on the Island of La Grande Jatte," which in turn inspired the musical *Sunday in the Park with George.* The other choices, Paul Signac and Charles Angrand, were also neo-impressionists who sometimes adopted Seurat's technique (as did Walter Hunt).

A4. c. Coe had written a mean-spirited song about Key West called "Jimmy Buffett Doesn't Live Here Anymore" and seemed hell-bent on deliberately attracting Jimmy's wrath, particularly since an earlier album already included "Divers Do It Deeper," a tastelessly off-color parody derived from "Changes in Latitudes, Changes in Attitudes."

A5.   e. Despite the album's title, Africa is the continent that Buffett is hovering over. For the phrase to have worked as a visual pun, he should have taken a step to the left and shimmied back a little bit.

A6.   a and c. Take 2 points for either and 5 points for both, but also subtract 2 points for each title that you shouldn't have picked. "The Good Fight" (b) by the way, was written with J.D. Souther while "Stars on the Water" was written by Rodney Crowell (without Jimmy Buffett's help).

A7.   d and e. Take 2 points for each right answer and 5 points for both. As an act of mercy, you may only subtract 1 point for each incorrect answer. Guy Lombardo and Richard Himber both had simultaneous hits with this song way back in 1934. For Guy Lombardo, it was one of his biggest hits—you may not realize this, but the man who was once king of those corny televised New Year's Eve parties was once quite huge, having more than two dozen no. 1 hits credited to him before the birth of rock and roll. Lombardo's version of "Stars Fell on Alabama" was a no. 1 hit for four weeks, while preventing Richard Himber's version of the same song from achieving the same status. Himber's no. 2 chart position represents the biggest hit of his career, which may explain why, over sixty years later, you've never heard of him.

By the way, do you realize that if you're *really, really* bad at this trivia stuff, you might end up with a negative score?

A8.   a through d is correct. Of all the names on the list, Ol' Blue Eyes is the only guy who didn't record a version of the song (though I can't say for sure that he never performed it). Take 5 points if you had all the correct names, or 1 point for each correct choice. Subtract a point if you had Frank on your list.

A9.   c. At the time, he was visiting the set to see his old friend Elizabeth Ashley.

A10. d. Jimmy Buffet (c), or as he pronounces it, "Boo-Fay," is the "T"-less vocalist who sings "Slow Boat to China" on *Somewhere Over China*. The other choices are just ridiculous.

A11. c

A12. c. Fredonia (a) is a name I lifted from a Marx Brothers movie (*Coconuts*) about another fictional independent state. The name was taken from an upstate college town in New York, near Buffalo and the Great Lakes. Margaritaville (b) was the "alternate" name utilized by the Conch Republic and Yoknapatawpha (d) is an imaginary county that appears in the literature of William Faulkner. It is also the name for the conference that is held in his honor.

A13. A "thirty-two hop" is a craps bet that says the dice will come up 3 and 2. A ten dollar "yo" is a $10 bet that the dice will come up 11.

A14. William Faulkner (3 points.), "Mosquitoes" (2 points)

A15. b

A16. c. The video itself is fairly painful to watch nowadays, due to its ridiculous storyboard, but serious fans may consider it worth seeing if for no other reason than to see Buffett doing a barefoot softshoe inside a gigantic top hat while wearing shorts and a crimson sports jacket. In most scenes, he is accompanied by a "Mr. Bojangles" type who magically transforms ordinary folks into white-tuxed hoofers.

A17. c. a and b are both credited to Buffett-Goodman, while d is written exclusively by Goodman. "Incommunicado" is credited to Buffett, background vocalist Deborah McColl, and percussionist M. L. Benoit.

A18. b. "Livin' It Up" was written with Josh Leo and J. D. Souther. The others are Buffett-Utley except "When the Wild Life Betrays Me," which is Buffett-Utley-Jennings.

A19. "...faux pas." This is one of my favorite Buffett puns (by now you may have noticed my tendency to consider most puns as the bane of all humor) in one of my favorite Buffett songs ("Twelve Volt Man"), but most people simply presume him to sing the number 'four' and then sigh in frustration. Take five points for "faux pas," but if you thought it was "four" and a sigh, take two points, since it at least proves that you're familiar with the lyrics.

A20. "...Someone call a decent physician," from "Growing Older but Not Up"

A21. b

A22. c

A23. c. "It's My Job" was released as a single but reached no higher than no. 57. It would be Buffett's last single to ever reach the pop charts.

A24. a. Although Buffett would eventually develop a mutually beneficial relationship with Corona beer, that wouldn't take place for another few years.

A25. d. The title came about due to Irving Azoff's ongoing feud with MCA Records. Since he was thoroughly frustrated with what he perceived to be the label's ineptitude, he advised his client (Buffett) to ready a final release for the label. *The Dog Ate My Homework and Other Great Excuses* became the working title for the upcoming sessions. After the fallout, Azoff found himself ensconced at the head of the label. This essentially put an end to the feud, since one of the few people who Azoff did not find it necessary to argue with was himself.

A26. b. Nesmith was one of the first artists to utilize video as an artistic and promotional medium for the home market—his *Elephant Parts* video collection (a) pre-dated MTV by more than five years. *Doctor Duck's Super Secret All-Purpose Sauce* came about a few years later and featured such upcoming comic talent as Jerry Seinfeld,

Whoopi Goldberg, Gary Shandling, Bob Goldthwaite, and Jay Leno. *Repo Man* (c) was the name of a movie that was handled by Nesmith's production company and which featured Buffett in a very small cameo appearance.

A27. b

A28. c. According to the lyrics, "It's Hump Day on the island. The lines have all gone dead" and as anybody who works from Monday to Friday ought to know, Wednesday is Hump Day.

A29. c

A30. b. The banker in the song (d. was more of a worrier than an optimist.

A31. c-1 ("I'm no Pete Rose..."), b-2 ("Now on the day that John Wayne died..."), a-3 (What in the hell did Marco Polo think when he ran into the wall..."), d-4 ("Hey, hey, Gardner McKay, take me on the Leaky Tiki..."), and e-5.

A32. b

A33. c

A34. d

A35. c. Like I said, I can't explain this dedication at all, unless it's a reference to what he was shooting for with the song's rhythm. d would have made a lot more sense, but "Creola" didn't appear on *Somewhere Over China*.

A36. "The Good Fight"

A37. R's and G's.

A38. a

A39. a

A40. a, b, and c. I'm willing to bet the farm that almost nobody got this question right, but yes, Buffett's fictional character from *Where Is Joe Merchant?*, Frank Bama, does indeed get credit as a backing vocalist here, while Tim Schmit does not. It's a fine line between fact and fiction, isn't it?

Score Results

0–80 points—Uh-oh. I doubt that you've gotten this far into the book without figuring that you knew what you were doing, only to discover that you're scoring in the bottom third. What happened? Ooh, you must be mad, figuring that these cock-amamie questions are too stupid for anybody to know. Well, you might be right (God knows I thought so when I was coming up with them), but I'll bet that plenty of Parrot Heads scored just fine. I'll tell you what—chill out, relax, and move on. Maybe you'll do better on the next section (though I doubt it!).

81–140 points—Not bad, but I'd bet you thought you'd do better. If I didn't write the test myself, I probably would've scored around here too, so don't feel too bad. Some of these questions might have fooled Jimmy Buffett himself. As for the next two sections, good luck.

141–200 points—Wow. I am truly impressed, because this section required not only specific "Buffett" knowledge but some diversity as well. Not only are you a Parrot Head, but you may also be a genius. The next two sections will help straighten that point out.

5

The Late Eighties

Anyone familiar with the lifespans of popular artists will note that with very few exceptions, those who rise to the top of the heap will soon be headed for a fall. Buffett proved to be no exception to this rule, and he was intelligent enough to see it coming. The trend for each of his albums to outsell the previous release had reversed in the first half of the eighties, and Buffett knew that something would have to be done if he planned to maintain his lifestyle. It was only natural to assume that his career might be headed toward the rocks, so he took action to steer himself away from anything quite so dangerous.

His first order of business was to increase his hold on the fans who remained faithful to him through the recent changes. A simple T-shirt business that he started with a member of his road crew was doing so well that he decided to open shop down in Key West and sell merchandise over the counter. At just about the same time, he also started a newsletter, known as the *Coconut Telegraph*, which served the dual purpose of keeping his fans informed of upcoming events and giving them easy access to the retail products that he offered in his store. The store and the mail-order business flourished. Soon, the T-shirt store would be expanded to a full-blown nightclub-restaurant-souvenir stand while paid subscriptions to the newsletter (it now costs $10 for an annual subscription, unless you buy merchandise) would increase exponentially.

With so many fans on the mailing list, they were only too happy to embrace the fun atmosphere of Buffett's escapist-tinged style. Many took on the goofy, tropical-based look that was being hawked in the Key West-based newsletter while others let their imaginations get the best of them and they exaggerated things to the point of extremism. Buffett's followers were now no longer simply fans. As the eighties wore on, Buffett fans were being transformed into Parrot Heads. As the eighties became the nineties, Buffett was once again on top. While most purveyors of mainstream popular culture remained blissfully unaware of Buffett's return to form, album sales started to improve while his ever-increasing army of dedicated followers made him one of the nation's top-grossing annual concert acts. He also came through on his commitment to write, penning a children's book called *The Jolly Mon* with his daughter Savannah Jane and a bestselling collection of short stories called *Tales From Margaritaville*. Albums that were released during Buffett's commercial rebirth include:

Last Mango in Paris	1985
Songs You Know By Heart	1985
Floridays	1986
Hot Water	1988
Off to See the Lizard	1989

Buffett also released a home video entitled

Jimmy Buffett Live by the Bay	1986

THE QUIZ

Q1. On the back cover of *Last Mango in Paris*, JB is standing
     on the bow of a rowboat, surrounded by swamp grass and
     reeds. With him is a buxom babe carrying an automatic
     weapon (it's a casual shot—just a day in the life). What is
     the registration that is airbrushed onto the boat's bow?
     a. MARG-4
     b. BYOB
     c. GYPSY-1
     d. OOTSK-1

Q2. *Last Mango in Paris* is dedicated to
     a. Jane and Savannah Jane
     b. His parents
     c. Bill Williams
     d. Steve Goodman

Q3. On what song does Buffett intone "skaters reverse" before
     the instrumental break?
     a. "The Perfect Partner"
     b. "Desperation Samba"
     c. "Please Bypass This Heart"
     d. "Frank and Lola"

Q4. In "You'll Never Work in Dis Bidness Again," who played
     the role of the ethnic (and unethical) business manager?
     a. Jimmy Buffett
     b. Josh Leo
     c. Matt Betton
     d. Vince Melamed

Adios, multiple choice. Once again, either you know the answer
or you don't.

Q5. For most of the *Live by the Bay* performance, Buffett's
     salmon-colored T-shirt is partially covered by his guitar
     and strap. Nonetheless, observant Parrot Heads will have
     figured out what is written across his chest. Tell me.

Q6. Who is Buffett's coauthor for the song "I Love the Now?"

Q7. Jimmy's conga player, Sam Clayton, was a member of what band throughout the '70s?

Q8. In 1989, Jimmy Buffett was in New Orleans to assist the Neville Brothers with a cable TV special. The show's production resembled a small-scaled version of Martin Scorcese's *The Last Waltz* (which featured the Band), with the Nevilles playing a few of their own songs while juggling various guests. Other than Buffett, special guests included John Hiatt, Bonnie Raitt, Dennis Quaid, Buckwheat Zydeco, Greg Allman, the Dirty Dozen Brass Band, the Dixie Cups and Daniel Lanois. With so many artists contributing career-defining performances, Buffett's bit is not one of the high points, but he at least holds his own ground among this phenomenally talented crew. What song did he perform with the Nevilles for this concert/film?

Q9. Which song does Jimmy Buffett explain thusly: "I would like to thank J. D. Souther for the book, Harry Belafonte for the early inspiration, and Mark Twain for taking the trip long ago"?

Q10. Since we've mentioned J. D. Souther, Steven Spielberg produced a film at the start of 1990 that features him performing a rendition of "Smoke Gets in Your Eyes" in an airplane hangar. It stars Richard Dreyfus, Holly Hunter, and John Goodman, with Audrey Hepburn making a special appearance as an angel (she was typecast). The soundtrack for this film also contains Buffett's "Boomerang Love" (mixed way, way back), as well as Bonnie Raitt ("Nick of Time"), the Platters ("Smoke Gets in Your Eyes"), Van Morrison ("Crazy Love"), and the Coasters ("Yakkety Yak"). Name the film.

And now, back to multiple choice:

Q11. When did the first Margaritaville store open?
    a. January '85   c. February '87
    b. January '86   d. July '87

Q12. Before the song "Prince of Tides," there existed a novel with the same title that was turned into a movie by Barbra Streisand, who produced and directed the film, and even starred in it (yeesh). Who wrote the book?
   a. John D. MacDonald
   b. Peter Mathiessen
   c. Pat Conroy
   d. Joe Giovinno

Q13. What famous '90s female vocalist sings back-up on *Off to See the Lizard?*
   a. Bonnie Raitt
   b. Alanis Morrisette
   c. Sheryl Crow
   d. Shawn Colvin

Q14. What cryptic phrase is written on the CD insert (or LP inner sleeve) of *Floridays?*
   a. "Bottom of the ninth, two out with a full count"
   b. "A day late and a dollar short"
   c. "Never eat anything bigger than your head"
   d. "Fifteen down and one to go"

Q15. Which of the following songs were not written by Buffett?
   a. "If It All Falls Down"
   b. "Mermaid in the Night"
   c. "Great Heart"
   d. "The Perfect Partner"

Q16. In the beginning of their affiliation with Buffett (1984), Corona Beer could account for 2 percent of the US import beer market. What could they boast just five years later?
   a. 2.5 percent, a 25 percent increase
   b. 3 percent, a 50 percent increase
   c. 6 percent, a 300 percent increase
   d. 17 percent, an 850 percent increase

Q17. Which album contains the following dedication; "This album is dedicated to John D. MacDonald, one of America's great natural resources"?
   a. Off to See the Lizard
   b. Hot Water

    c. Floridays

    d. Last Mango in Paris

Q18. "The time has come," the walrus said
and little oysters hide their head...

Buffett places this couplet into a verse of "That's What Livin' Is to Me." Who wrote it, and where did it originally appear?

    a. Lewis Carroll, *Alice in Wonderland*

    b. Lewis Carroll, *Through the Looking Glass, and What Alice Found There*

    c. Mark Twain, *A Connecticut Yankee in King Arthur's Court*

    d. Mark Twain, *The Adventures of Huckleberry Finn*

Q19. Immediately following the above couplet, Buffett goes on as follows:

    My Twain of thought is loosely bound.
    I guess it's time...

Finish the phrase.

Q20. In 1987, Buffett went to Australia to witness the Americas Cup yachting race. He even wrote a song for the occasion, a single that would crop up on *Boats, Beaches, Bars, and Ballads*. It was called "Take it Back." Did we?

Q21. Each of the following songs were chosen for the soundtrack of a movie except one. Choose the song that was not used in a movie.

    a. "Ragtop Day"

    b. "Turning Around"

    c. "Take It Back"

    d. "Don't Bug Me"

Points for the next three questions are all or nothing:

Q22. Arrange the running of the following songs from side one of *Last Mango in Paris*.

    a. "The Perfect Partner"

    b. "Gypsies in the Palace"

    c. "Frank and Lola"

    d. "Everybody's On the Run"

    e. "Please Bypass This Heart"

Q23. Let's do the same thing for the songs on side one of the *Hot Water* LP.

    a. "Prince of Tides"

    b. "Bring Back the Magic"

    c. "Baby's Gone Shoppin'"

    d. "Homemade Music"

    e. "My Barracuda"

    f. "L'Air de la Louisiane"

Q24. How about side two of *Last Mango in Paris?*

    a. "Desperation Samba"

    b. "Last Mango in Paris"

    c. "If the Phone Doesn't Ring, It's Me"

    d. "Jolly Mon Sing"

    e. "Beyond the End"

Q25. True or False: The parenthetical title of "Desperation Samba" is "(Halloween in Mexico)."

Q26. True or False: Buffett is wearing the same hat (the one with the "heart on the wing" pin attached) for both the *Hot Water* and the *Off to See the Lizard* photo shoots.

Q27. True or False: Buffett can be seen wearing two earrings in his left lobe on the front and back cover of *Hot Water*. One of the earrings is in the shape of a single ivory die (the singular of dice).

Q28. True or False: The bullwhip cracks on "Desperation Samba" were recorded by Harrison Ford in Soundtrack Recording Studio in Jackson Hole, Wyoming.

Q29. The gun-toting babe featured on the back cover of the *Last Mango in Paris* album is also prominent on the front cover for the more formal restaurant shot. The photo is unusual in that it is one of the very few shots of Buffett wearing a tie. What is his dining partner grasping in her left hand?

    a. A menu

  b. A wine list
  c. The bill—I guess she's paying
  d. A gold revolver

Q30. The conversation in "Last Mango in Paris" takes place at Captain Tony's Saloon. Who is Jimmy talking to?
  a. Phil Clark
  b. The owner of the bar, Tony Tarracino
  c. It's an imaginary conversation with Hemingway
  d. Buffett is talking to a reflection of himself in his old age.

Q31. Jimmy's "First Look" takes place where?
  a. Rio de Janeiro, Brazil
  b. Paris, France
  c. Papeete, Tahiti
  d. Havana, Cuba

Q32. What Buffett song mentions Otis Redding's "Dock of the Bay," then incorporates its trademark whistle during the fade-out?
  a. "My Barracuda"
  b. "The Perfect Partner"
  c. "Meet Me in Memphis"
  d. "Why the Things We Do"

Q33. Where did Frank and Lola take their second honeymoon?
  a. Key West
  b. The Bahamas
  c. Miami
  d. Pensacola

Q34. According to the lyrics of this same song, Frank and Lola spend a lot of time eating while trying to reinvigorate their marriage. Which of the following foods does not appear in the lyrics as part of their diet?
  a. Junior mints
  b. A dozen oysters
  c. Burgers with the works
  d. Popcorn

Q35. Jimmy Buffett wrote or cowrote all the songs on *Floridays* except one. Which?

    a. "If It All Falls Down"

    b. "Meet Me in Memphis"

    c. "Creola"

    d. "I Love the Now"

Q36. Auntie Mae, Papa T, and cousin Mabel make a guest appearance in the lyrics of which song?

    a. "Pascagoula Run"

    b. "Frank and Lola"

    c. "Creola"

    d. "Life is Just a Tire Swing"

Q37. Match the geographical location with the song that mentions it (all titles are culled from *Floridays*)

    a. Leblon   1. "Floridays"

    b. Ramrod Key 2. "Meet Me in Memphis"

    c. Beirut   3. "First Look"

    d. Biloxi   4. "You'll Never Work in Dis Business Again"

Q38. Jimmy Buffett covered one song that was written by Johnny Clegg. What was the title of the song?

    a. "King of Somewhere Hot"

    b. "Great Heart"

    c. "Beyond the End"

    d. "Gravity Storm"

Q39. What song was inspired by a conversation that Buffett overheard in an elevator?

Q40. One song from "Hot Water" ends with Buffett quietly saying thank you at song's end. What song is it?

THE ANSWERS

A1. d is correct. This isn't as obscure as it seems. If you let it sink in, you'll realize that OOTSK stands for the Order of the Sleepless Knights.

A2. d again. Unlike almost every other album, this record is not dedicated to his family. Bill Williams (c) was the recipient of a dedication on *Somewhere Over China* (Williams was Buffett's old boss at *Billboard* magazine) but *Last Mango in Paris* is dedicated to Steve Goodman, who had passed away that year. He is also credited as Buffett's songwriting partner for "Frank and Lola" (published two years earlier, before Goodman's sickness had overwhelmed him). The credit reads "This album is dedicated with fond memories to one of the finest humans who ever spent time on this planet—STEVE GOODMAN. I regret that his stay was so short. I miss you."

A3. c

A4. d. On this track, Melamed expanded his role as the "other" keyboard player (after Utley, of course) in this two man miniplay.

A5. "Only visiting this planet"

A6. The one and only Princess Leia of *Star Wars* fame, Paul Simon's ex, Carrie Fisher.

A7. Sam Clayton became a member of Little Feat on their third album, *Dixie Chicken*. He also appeared on their classic albums *Feats Don't Fail Me Now*, *The Last Record Album*, *Time Loves a Hero*, and *Waiting for Columbus*, among others. He remained with the band until Lowell George's untimely death, and has also rejoined them now that they are recording and touring with Craig Fuller (ex–Pure Prairie League) in George's place.

A8. "Middle of the Night." This song remained unreleased until the *Boats Beaches, Bars, and Ballads* box set, which includes a studio recording of this title. The song was written by Buffett, Utley, and Jennings in conjunction with Art Neville. In the same video performance, Buffett later joins the stage with the entire cast and crew for a rousing version of "Fire on the Bayou."

A9. "That's What Livin' Is to Me," from *Hot Water*

A10. "Always"

A11. a

A12. c

A13. c

A14. d. This was probably a reference to his recording contract, and a not too subtle dig at MCA, who would soon be renegotiating new terms with Buffett.

A15. a through d are all correct. None of them were written by Buffett. a was written by Matt Betton, b by Jay Oliver and Roger Guth, c by Johnny Clegg, and d by Marshall Chapman. Take 1 point for each choice you recognized, and take all 5 points if you knew he didn't write any of these choices.

A16. d (!). Besides tequila, I guess Parrot Heads drink an awful lot of beer, too.

A17. b, *Hot Water*

A18. b is the closest correct answer. The first line is an exact duplication of a line in Carroll's poem as it appears in *Through the Looking Glass*, while the second line more or less summarizes the plight of the oysters. If you have kids, read this to them. It must qualify as one of the most imaginatively beautiful children's stories of all time, and you'll probably find yourself enjoying it as much as the kids.

A19. "...to Mark this down." This is another squeamish pun that plays with Samuel Clemens's pen name in order to make a point about the perils of keeping a journal.

A20. As a matter of fact, yes we did. If you didn't know this, the Americas Cup race is named for a schooner that won the trophy back in 1851, but it might as well have been named for the country itself, since the New York Yacht Club had never, *never*, lost possession of the trophy—that is not until 1983, when the Australians were the first challenger in history to usurp the Americans. Bent on avenging his embarrassment as the first American to not win, Dennis Conner captained *Stars and Stripes* against Australia's *Kookaburra III* and did indeed "Take it Back."

A21. c. a appeared in *The Slugger's Wife,* while b was used for *Summer Rental* and d was written for *Arachnophobia.*

A22. d, c, a, e, b

A23. d, c, b, e, f, a

A24. a, c, b, d, e

A25. False, it should read "(Halloween in Tijuana)."

A26. False. He wears the "heart on the wing" pin for the *Hot Water* photos, but the *Last Mango in Paris* shots feature Buffett wearing either a salmon-colored baseball cap with what appears to be a fish pin on the back cover and a black beret with a lizard pin on the cover photo.

A27. True. The album credits even mention the earring designer, Lise Ireland.

A28. True

A29. d. Although it's difficult to make out from the angle of the camera lens, the mirror next to the table clearly reveals that her penchant for guns is not abated while dining. By the way, although it's not directly credited as the location, I'm reasonably certain from my own New Orleans culinary experiences that this photo was taken inside the world famous French Quarter restaurant on Bourbon Street known as Galatoire's.

A30. b

A31. a

A32. c

A33. d

A34. c

A35. a. Strangely, although it wasn't written by Buffett, "If It All Falls Down" appears to be one of the more autobiographical songs he ever recorded. Whether it's true, as the lyrics suggest, that he never passed his S.A.T.'s is uncertain (if not unlikely), but it is probably safe to say that Buffett comfortably fits the bill of being a "hard drinking calypso poet."

A36. c

A37. a-3, b-2, c-1, and d-4.

A38. b

A39. "Pre You." While in an elevator, Buffett overheard one enlisted man telling another about meeting an ex-lover when he was out with his current date. When asked how he got out of the sticky situation, he responded by saying "I told her that she was 'pre-you.'—4"

A40. "That's What Living Is to Me." The song also ends the album.

Score Results

0–100 points—I know what you're thinking. This section was absolutely ridiculous. Nobody could have gotten half of these questions right. Well, look at the bright side—see how much you've learned? And, you should be comforted to know that I expect at least half of the people who try this test to score in this range, so you're in good company.

101–150 points—Well, I've got to hand it to you, because if you've scored this well, then you're bound to qualify as a Parrot Head. It might not seem as though you did so great, but this section was *tough*. Good going.

151–200 points—Why are you wasting your time with this book when you could be perfecting your theories on genetic research?

6

The Nineties

By anybody's standard, the nineties have been an extremely busy and satisfying time for Jimmy Buffett. Practically every single plan that he put into action during the eighties to aid in his longevity worked better than even he could have predicted. It was an amazing feat, one that was unprecedented in the music industry, but Buffett returned to form, more popular and successful than ever. Best of all, he was conquering aspects of business and entertainment that most pop artists wouldn't even know where to begin. And he did all of this with no hit single since 1977's "Margaritaville."

His modest T-shirt business has erupted into two thriving restaurants/bars/nightclubs/souvenir stands, one in Key West and another in New Orleans. His clothing line flourishes, thanks mostly to his newsletter, whose subscription rate has soared. He has written two books, one a novel and the other a collection of short stories. Both were bestsellers. With his daughter Savannah Jane, he also authored two children's books. His Parrot Head fan base has grown exponentially also, funding virtually every project that Buffett attempts. Besides making his annual tours blockbuster events that continually gross in the top ten for income and attendance, Parrot Heads trust

Buffett to supply them with the type of entertainment that they desire, regardless of the medium. Most recently, this extended itself to a musical production of Herman Wouk's novel, *Don't Stop the Carnival*. Although Buffett did not appear onstage during the production, fans "phlocked" to hear his music performed by a professional cast and pit band.

As of this writing, it remains quite feasible that this show will go on tour until it has a few of the kinks ironed out and then...Broadway! In addition, his official Web site, Jimmy Buffett's Margaritaville, has become one of the most popular stops in cyberspace. From any angle, it seems that Buffett has aligned himself into a position where virtually every marketable idea is not only feasible, but likely to succeed.

One disappointment among these successes was the outcome of Buffett's boutique label, Margaritaville Records. The record company was started with the intention of providing fans of Buffett's music easy access to other acts that he hoped would appeal to Parrot Heads. By deliberately avoiding high-profile artists and concentrating instead on acts that were more appropriately suited to a smaller label with modest ambitions, Margaritaville Records was established with the intention of being profitable, but not at the expense of changing the label's original charter. Distribution was originally handled by MCA, then later transferred to Island. Unfortunately, most acts sold less than was hoped for, causing the label staff, and eventually its roster of artists, to be pared down. At present, it appears as though Margaritaville Records will soon cease to exist altogether.

Commercial enterprises that aided Buffett in his steady climb include a live album, his first since 1978, and a boxed-set career retrospective, which has earned the distinction of being the best-selling boxed-set in history. Various songs were contributed to major soundtracks, including *Arachnophobia*, where a song was written to spec for the movie, and *The Doctor*, which utilized an old chestnut from his catalog ("Why Don't We Get Drunk") as a central theme. His involvement in film also extended to standing in front of the camera, with small acting roles in the movies *Cobb* and *Congo*. CD releases that took place during this part of Buffett's career include

Jimmy Buffett Live! Feeding Frenzy	1990
Boats, Beaches, Bars, and Ballads	1992
Fruitcakes	1993
Barometer Soup	1995
Banana Wind	1996
Christmas Island	1996

QUIZ TIME

Q1. Who starred in *Arachnophobia?*
   a. Alec Baldwin
   b. Michael Douglas
   c. Jeff Daniels
   d. Jeff Goldblum

Q2. In 1989, Buffett and his daughter Savannah Jane made a trip to Africa, one of the few parts of the world he had yet to see. This trip would later serve as the inspiration for a short story that was contributed to *Heaven is Under Our Feet—A Book for Walden Woods*. What was the title of this story?
   a. "Everything in the Woods Wants to Eat a Quail (Including Me)"
   b. "It's Nearly Africa"
   c. "The End of More"
   d. "A Boxful of Africa"
   e. "Six String Music"

Q3. What song does Buffett sing with Frank Sinatra?
   a. "Mack the Knife"
   b. "Come Fly With Me"
   c. "Margaritaville"
   d. "Witchcraft"

Q4. Other than Buffett himself, who was the first act signed to Margaritaville Records?
   a. The Iguanas
   b. Marshall Chapman
   c. Fingers Taylor
   d. Evangeline

Q5. The offices of Margaritaville Records are (or were) located in...
   a. Key West
   b. New Orleans
   c. Nashville
   d. Los Angeles

Q6. What was the first release on Margaritaville?
   a. Evangeline's eponymous debut CD
   b. *Jimmy Buffett Live! Feeding Frenzy*
   c. The Iguanas' debut CD
   d. *Boats, Beaches, Bars, and Ballads*

Q7. The Book *Heaven Is Under Our Feet* contains a Buffett essay, along with many others. How many of the below-named celebrities, actors, musicians, writers, etc. also contributed? Choose all that apply.
   a. Carrie Fisher
   b. Kurt Vonnegut
   c. Norman Mailer
   d. Tom Cruise
   e. Jimmy Carter
   f. Paula Abdul
   g. Barbra Streisand
   h. Glenn Frey

Q8. This question is so obscure that even I can't believe it: My own African friend, a South African native, points out that the term for their currency is misspelled on the lyric sheet to "Bank of Bad Habits." It reads "kruggerand." What is the correct spelling?

Q9. In 1996, Jimmy Buffett attended an auction at Sotheby's in Manhattan for the estate of Jacqueline Kennedy Onassis.

While there, he made a few successful bids, including a $9,200 purchase of a guest list containing the signatures of Jacqueline Kennedy and Lady Bird Johnson. What else did he buy?

    a. A jeweled cigar box that sat on John Kennedy's desk

    b. A collection of leather-bound books that once sat in John Kennedy's office

    c. A Jamie Wyeth lithograph of JFK in a sailboat

    d. A set of golf clubs that belonged to JFK

Q10. "Domino College" was written by Jimmy Buffett and...

    a. Michael Utley

    b. Joe Walsh

    c. Glenn Frey

    d. Dan Fogelberg

    e. Peter Mayer

Q11. Match the song title from *BBBB* with the album it was originally intended for (or the sessions that spawned it):

    a. "Elvis Imitators"   1. *Feeding Frenzy*

    b. "Everlasting Moon"   2. *Hot Water*

    c. "Domino College"   3. *Somewhere Over China*

    d. "Love and Luck"   4. *Floridays*

Q12. Has anybody else besides me noticed how often Buffett's soundtrack appearances accompany truck-stop scenes from their respective movies? All but one of the following songs appeared in movie scenes that take place in trucks and/or truck stops. Which is the exception?

    a. "Ragtop Day"—*The Slugger's Wife*

    b. "Stars on the Water"—*The Firm*

    c. "Survive"—*Coast to Coast*

    d. "Boomerang Love"—*Always*

Q13. Regarding Buffett's appearance on *Kermit UnPigged:* In typical fashion that causes most Parrot Heads to have a fit resembling a seizure, Rizzo the Rat mistakenly reads Jimmy Buffett's name as "Jimmy's Buffet," dropping the last *t* and thus assuming that he happened upon a banquet. When he discovers his mistake, he decides that he'll go down the hall to check in on another performer. Who?

Q14. What is (or are) DRALS (or drals)?
    a. An acronym for Disco, Rap, and Lip-Synch
    b. A dorsal fin on a tiger shark
    c. An acronym for the Drugs, Rock 'n' roll And Liquor Society
    d. Those things at the end of your shoelaces

Q15. Which of the following artists did *not* write a sad song entitled "Souvenirs"?
    a. Paul McCartney
    b. John Prine
    c. Dan Fogelberg
    d. James Taylor
    e. Danny O'Keefe
    f. Jimmy Buffett

Q16. In the liner notes to *Fruitcakes*, Buffett mentions an old friend for whom he used to serve as an opening act, a musician-performer who inspired him to perfect his own brand of storytelling, music, and humor. Who is he?
    a. Leon Gamble
    b. Kenny Rogers
    c. Leon Rogers
    d. Gamble Rogers
    e. Leon Russell
    f. Lord Buckley

Q17. Who plays drums on James Taylor's original recording of "Mexico"?
    a. Russ Kunkel
    b. Roger Guth
    c. Matt Betton
    d. Sammy Creason

Q18. Match the song title with the author whose story inspired it (one author must be used twice).
    a. "Barometer Soup"   1. Jim Harrison
    b. "Remittance Man"   2. F. Scott
    c. "Diamond as Big as the   Fitzgerald
       Ritz"   3. Mark Twain

    d. "Lage Nom Ai"   4. Carl Hiaasen
    e. "Ballad of Skip Wiley"

Q19. In my opinion, I don't think enough has been said about Peter Mayer's influence on Buffett's music since *Off to See the Lizard*. He's a brilliant musician who is largely responsible for many of the adventurous directions that the Coral Reefer band has taken in the '90s. When not touring or recording with Buffett, Mayer also has his own band. What is the band's name?

Q20. On Evangeline's debut disc, Buffett assisted by supplying background vocals to one song on the collection. What was the name of the song?

Q21. In the midst of the live version of "You'll Never Work in Dis Bidness Again," the Coral Reefers launch into an improbable parody of a classic rock staple. For three points, what song is it and for another two points, who wrote the song and had the original hit?

Q22. Speaking of the live album, Buffett recorded two songs for this collection that were not previously released in a studio version. One is Mac McAnally's "In the City." For three points, what is the other unreleased song, and for the last two points, who had the original hit with this song back in the late fifties?

Q23. What Buffett record achieved the highest pop chart position of his entire career, according to the various charts of *Billboard* magazine? I'm talking about any medium (i.e., single or album).
    a. "Margaritaville"
    b. *Fruitcakes*
    c. *Barometer Soup*
    d. *Banana Wind*

Q24. Match the release with its highest chart position (two albums had the same peak spot, so you'll have to use one figure twice).
    a. *Feeding Frenzy*   1. No. 4
    b. *Boats, Beaches, Bars, and*   2. No. 5
       Ballads   3. No. 6

    c. *Fruitcakes*   4. No. 27
    d. *Barometer Soup*   5. No. 68
    e. *Banana Wind*
    f. *Christmas Island*

Q25. On the liner notes of 1980's *Coconut Telegraph*, Buffett mentions his nickname for the newborn Savannah Jane as "The Noop." According to magazine article quotes, what was Buffett's nickname for Sarah Delaney when she was an infant?

Q26. The man in charge of day-to-day operations at Margaritaville Records is named Bob Mercer. Besides being a onetime manager of ex-Beatle Paul McCartney, Mercer was once employed by England's EMI Records, where he was responsible for signing and promoting which of the following acts?
    a. Queen
    b. Pink Floyd
    c. The Sex Pistols
    d. The Clash

Q27. On the title track from *Fruitcakes*, Buffett expends an awful lot of energy yelling about Junior Mints. What previous Buffett recording also happens to mention Junior Mints?

Q28. According to Jimmy's version of "Another Saturday Night," if he doesn't find a honey to help him spend his money, what's he gonna do?
    a. "I'm prob'ly gonna lose my mind."
    b. "I'm headin' back to Key West town."
    c. "I'll jump in the river and drown."
    d. "I'm gonna have to blow this town."

Q29. Name the song from *Feeding Frenzy* that Buffett introduces thusly: "This is a song for all of you who have been with us for all of the years that we've been doing this, and we'll also do it for all of you people that weren't alive when this song was a hit."

Q30. According to Jimmy's rap on *Feeding Frenzy*'s "Today's Message," how much did he pay for his pickup truck back in the early Key West days?

Q31. In the interest of world peace, which of the following catalogs does Jimmy want to drop onto the now-defunct Soviet Union?
   a. L. L. Bean
   b. Disney
   c. Sporty's Pilot Shop
   d. Victoria's Secret
   e. Coldwater Creek
   f. Murray Brothers Fishing and Tackle of Palm Beach

Q32. On *Feeding Frenzy*, what song does Jimmy introduce as "the scariest song of the evening" (hint: it features Zachary Richard on Cajun accordion)?

Q33. Name three songs that were hits for other artists before Buffett decided to cover them on *Fruitcakes*. Then, name the artist who was responsible for them.

Q34. Buffett has been known to perform the occasional Beatles song in concert, but he has only recorded and released one song that was written by a Beatle. What's the song?

Q35. What is the secret track that crops up at the end of the *Banana Wind* collection? Name the song title and the artist who wrote it.

Q36. On *Banana Wind*, one song manages to somehow scramble references to Picasso, Manet, Hemingway, Hunter Thompson, Joan of Arc, the Village People (!), and the Rolling Stones. Name the song.

Q37. Back in the early eighties, Buffett teamed up now and then with Dave Loggins to write a song or two: "Treat Her Like a Lady" and "Island" appeared on *Volcano* and *Coconut Telegraph*, respectively. Another Buffett-Loggins composition crops up on *Banana Wind*. Which of the following songs was penned by this team?
   a. "Only Time Will Tell"

     b. "Holiday"
     c. "Happily Ever After (Now and Then)"
     d. "Schoolboy Heart"

Q38. Have you ever envied the lifestyle of a jellyfish? Buffett has, and he writes about it. What song contains this unusual lyrical thrust?
     a. "Cultural Infidel"
     b. "Mental Floss"
     c. "Lone Palm"
     d. "Overkill"

Q39. What song makes passing reference to grunge, sugar barons, the fox-trot, and barbeque?
     a. "Desdemona's Building a Rocket Ship"
     b. "Fruitcakes"
     c. "Everybody's Got a Cousin in Miami"
     d. "The Bob Roberts Society Band"

Q40. Match the geographical location with the song that mentions it.

a. Cayo Hueso	1. "Love in the Library"
b. Zanzibar	2. "Quietly Making Noise"
c. Champs Elysees	3. "Everybody's Got a Cousin in Miami"
d. Government and Bay Avenue	4. "Six String Music"
e. Laguna	5. "Frenchman For the Night"

ANSWERS

A1. c

A2. d. a is the name of an essay that he wrote for Esquire Magazine, b is the name of a song by the band XTC, and c is the name of Don Johnson's essay in the very same book. e is a song title from *Fruitcakes* that alludes to the same trip.

A3. a

A4. d. Evangeline can best be described as a five woman "Cajun-flavored" act. By the way, the Iguanas (a) were the second act signed.

A5. c. Its offices are located directly across the street from Margaritaville's parent label, MCA.

A6. d. It was an ambitious first release, since it was a four CD boxed set, but it was a practical decision as well. Buffett was stoking so many different fires that he was finding it difficult to make time to record a full set of new material, so he was hoping that the four-CD retrospective could work as a holding pattern for fans who were growing restless for new product. It was a wise commercial decision, too, since it has since grown to be one of the most successful boxed sets ever released.

A7. All but (c) Norman Mailer, (g) Barbra Streisand, and (h) Glenn Frey contributed essays. Take one point for each correct choice, and subtract a point for any wrong guess.

A8. The correct spelling for this word is "krugerrand." Hey, if Parrot Heads can get so excited about Buffett's name requiring two *t*s, then the same should apply for krugerrand's two *r*s, right?

A9. c. Buffett paid $43,700 for the lithograph. As an additional point of information, Buffett attended another auction in 1997 where he reportedly was the successful bidder on a collection of leather-bound books by former President Jimmy Carter. As for the golf clubs, I seem to recall a Seinfeld episode revolving around Kramer's possession of a set of JFK-owned golf clubs.

A10. d

A11. a-3, b-1, c-4, d-2. 1 point for each correct answer, 5 points if you matched them all

A12. d. The scene for this song took place in airplane hanger.

A13. Meat Loaf. When Gonzo asks him if there was any food left, he responds, "Nah. There was some big guy in there. I guess he ate it all."

A14. a. On one of his tours, Jimmy took to showing a short film during intermission which left little doubt as to where his opinion stood regarding certain "noncompatible" musical styles. As an update of the xenophobic opinion of disco that was held by many rock fans, Jimmy expanded this prejudice to encompass rap music, as well as the tendency for some pop artists to fake their vocals over prerecorded tracks (remember Milli Vanilli?). He did this by holding up a sign with the universal restriction symbol (a red circle with a slash) over the acronym DRALS. Done in the style of a World War II newsreel, it featured Buffett dogfighting the evil forces of "DRALS" with a cameo appearance by actor Harrison Ford as Indiana Jones. By the way, have you listened to the song "Overkill" from *Banana Wind* lately? No "rap," indeed.

A15. a, d, and f are correct, although Paul McCartney did write a sad song about souvenirs called "Junk" for his first solo album. Prine and Fogelberg both have career-defining tunes with this title, while Danny O'Keefe and synth player Vince Melamed (not mentioned above for fear of giving the question away a bit too obviously) teamed up to write the song that Buffett performs on *Late Night Menu.*

A16. d. Buffett dedicates *Fruitcakes* to Gamble Rogers, who had passed away the previous year while trying to rescue a drowning victim.

A17. a. Buffett's producer Russ Kunkel did a load of session work for California-based artists throughout the '70s and '80s. For Buffett's version, Kunkel got to sit behind the Neve soundboard instead of his drum kit.

A18. a-3, b-3, c-2, d-1, e-4. Take one point for each correct match.

A19. PM. The band consists of his brother, Jim Mayer, on bass and Roger Guth on drums. Both are also members of Buffett's Coral Reefers.

A20. "Gulf Coast Highway"

A21. "Foxy Lady," by Jimi Hendrix (the Reeferettes sing "Foxy Bubba")

A22. In 1956, Harry Belafonte had a substantial hit with "Jamaica Farewell."

A23. d. Believe it or not, "Margaritaville" would be in last place among these four choices. Excluding Buffett's Christmas album, his past four studio albums each debuted in the top 10—*Banana Wind* at no. 4, *Fruitcakes* at no. 5, and *Barometer Soup* at no. 6. The 45 of "Margaritaville" was Buffett's highest charting 45, and it reached no. 8.

A24. a-5, b-5, c-2, d-3, e-1, f-4. Take a point for each correct match, but take no more than five points total!

A25. "The Pud"

A26. All but d. Take one point for each correct choice and take 5 points if you answered the question 100 percent correct.

A27. "Frank and Lola" ("The Junior Mints were mushy but the sex was neat.")

A28. b. Buffett's recording of this song can be found on the first *Margaritaville Cafe* album.

A29. "Come Monday"

A30. One hundred bucks.

A31. a, c, and d is the only correct answer. Got it right, take 5 points. If you guessed any other combination, don't take anything.

A32. "Gypsies in the Palace"

A33. "Uncle John's Band," by the Grateful Dead, "Sunny Afternoon," by the Kinks and "She's Got You," by Patsy Cline. Take a point for each song-artist combination you could muster, 5 points if you knew them all.

A34. "Happy Christmas (War Is Over)," by John Lennon and Yoko Ono.

A35. "Treetop Flier," written by Stephen Stills. Take 2 points for the song title only, five if you knew the author as well.

A36. The aptly titled "Cultural Infidel."

A37. c

A38. b

A39. d

A40. a-3, b-4, c-5, d-1, e-2.

Results, Anyone?

0–70 points—Were you out too late last night? I can't believe that you would have come so far only to do so poorly. Maybe you should take the test again, but only after the painkillers (and chocolate milk, orange juice, Darvon, etc.) take effect.

71–150 points—Old fans and newcomers alike tend to be intimately familiar with Buffett's recent material, so I would guess that you expected to do better than this. Hey, don't blame *me* for utilizing too many questions that are barely related to the subject at hand (I'll bet that "krugerrand" thing really teed you off). After all, you're the one who thought that you already knew it all.

151–200 points—Well, you did it. What more can I say? There's still the literature chapter, though (you'd better go read *Trouble Dolls*), not to mention the "ultimate" quiz. I'll trip you up yet (or get writer's cramp trying).

7

Buffett's Books

As a fan of Jimmy Buffett, you must know that besides being a talented musician, he is also a highly praised and successful writer. The question, though, isn't whether or not you know that he writes, it's whether or not you have read what he's written. This quiz is written to determine that you've taken time out from his music and concerts long enough to spend some time with his books (and maybe some cash on buying your own personal copies), then to see whether or not you were able to retain a healthy portion of the book's contents. This section covers two children's books and two more mature works. They are

The Jolly Mon (written with daughter Savannah Jane)	1988
Tales From Margaritaville	1989
Trouble Dolls (written with daughter Savannah Jane)	1991
Where is Joe Merchant?	1992

ONCE AGAIN, IT'S QUIZ TIME!

The following questions apply (mostly) to *Tales From Margaritaville.*

QI. Pick as many as five song titles from the following list of ten that also happen to be Buffett-penned story titles. Pick only what you're sure of. Add one point for each correct answer, but subtract a point for each wrong answer (there, that ought to keep you honest).

    a. "The Jolly Mon"
    b. "That's My Story and I'm Stickin' to It"
    c. "Last Mango in Paris"
    d. "The Pascagoula Run"
    e. "Mermaid in the Night"
    f. "Trouble Dolls"
    g. "Boomerang Love"
    h. "Carnival World"
    i. "Off to See the Lizard"
    j. "I Wish Lunch Could Last Forever"

Q2. Real or Unreal?—Assuming you have learned to accept the fact that there is no geographical island or town called Margaritaville (at least not yet—discounting the existence of someplace called Margarita Island off the coast of Venezuela. If you're an optimist, keep in mind that there was no such place as Key Largo, either, until after the Humphrey Bogart film), how about Jimmy's other constantly referred to locale, Snake Bite Key?

Q3. How about Heat Wave, Alabama?

Q4. Heartache, Wyoming?

Q5. The subtitle to *Tales From Margaritaville* is...
    a. *Fishy Tales and Broken Scales*
    b. *Fictional Fish and Fishy Fictions*
    c. *Fictional Facts and Factual Fictions*
    d. *Factually Fishy Fictions From Florida*

Q6. Which album title is also the title of a Buffett short story?
- a. *The Coconut Telegraph*
- b. *Floridays*
- c. *Last Mango in Paris*
- d. *Off to See the Lizard*

Q7. What is Mark Twain's quoted advice that kicks off the text and sets the tone for *Tales From Margaritaville?*

Q8. In one of the nonfictional stories, Buffett mentions the name of the three-room hotel/bar that he owned shares in (until it burnt down, that is), in spite of his familiarity with Herman Wouk's *Don't Stop the Carnival*. What was it?
- a. Le Select
- b. Autour Du Rochen
- c. Maison DeVille
- d. The Virgin Gorda

Q9. One intriguing story in *Tales From Margaritaville* concerns itself with Buffett's travel to Cuba and his encounter with Gregorio Fuentes, the real-life inspiration for Hemingway's *The Old Man and the Sea*. What is the name of this story?
- a. "Hooked in the Heart"
- b. "Life in the Food Chain"
- c. "A Gift for the Buccaneer"
- d. "Are You Ready for Freddy?"

The following two questions are concerned with the short story entitled "Off to See the Lizard":

Q10. What are the names of the identical twin sisters who own and operate the Northern Lights Cafe (first and last names, please)?

Q11. What was the name of the Heat Wave, Alabama high school football team that obsessed the twin sisters?

Q12. *Tales From Margaritaville* consists mostly of fictional tales, except for the book's last section, "Son of a Son of a Sailor," which contains nonfictional accounts. One story

from this section is called "Life in the Food Chain" and it
starts with Buffett describing a short sail with a friend
aboard Buffett's sloop, the Savannah Jane. What makes the
Savannah Jane unusual?

   a. She has no engine.

   b. She has a built-in recording studio.

   c. She has no electrical power.

   d. She sails poorly when heading toward weather.

Q13. In this same story, Buffett relates a tale where his grandfather was sailing with his family from the Turks and
Caicos Islands to New York, when the wind died and the
boat began to drift along with the tide. This situation
lasted for twenty-eight harrowing days, while food and
water supplies dissipated. The family came dangerously
close to severe dehydration and starvation until a passing
ship spotted them and gave them enough provisions to
survive until the wind once again cooperated. What is the
name of the boat that Buffett's family was sailing on when
this happened?

Q14. In the story "Are You Ready for Freddy?" what is the name
of the fictional rock 'n' roller that Buffett happened to
meet at "an old watering hole" named Alabama Jacks
while en route to Key West?

The following questions apply to *The Jolly Mon*.

Q15. What is the name of the dolphin in *The Jolly Mon?*

   a. Flipper

   b. Albion

   c. Orion

   d. Arion

Q16. What is the princess's name?

   a. Petunia

   b. Marigold

   c. Rosie

   d. Albion

Q17. Where did the Jolly Mon come from?
  a. Bananaland
  b. Coconut Island
  c. Parrot Key
  d. Lemonland
  e. Mango Bay

Q18. Before allowing her pirate gang to throw the chained Jolly Mon into the sea, One-Eyed Rosie demands that he play a song. What are the lines that Jolly Mon sings before being rudely interrupted by Rosie hollering "That's quite enough, Mr. Jolly Mon"?

Q19. Who is responsible for the instrumental backing that accompanies Jimmy and Savannah Jane's audio reading of *The Jolly Mon?*
  a. Michael Utley
  b. Matt Betton
  c. Peter Mayer
  d. Russ Kunkel

Q20. Fill in the blank from the inscription on back of the Jolly Mon's guitar: "Now go make your music in lands near and far; _____ protects you wherever you are."

The following questions apply to *Trouble Dolls*.

Q21. In *Trouble Dolls*, what is the name of Lizzy Rhinehart's dog?
  a. Spring
  b. Cheeseburger
  c. Spooner
  d. Summer

Q22. What's the name of her sailboat?
  a. The *Songbird*
  b. The *Savannah Jane*
  c. The *Parakeet*
  d. *Lady of the Waters*

Q23. The Trouble Dolls are named...
  a. Moe, Larry, Curly, and Shemp

  b. Julio, Esmerelda, Pedro, and Maria
  c. Tiny, Minnie, Penny, and Spot
  d. Big Blue, Little Red, Pinky, and Crusty

Q24. What is Lizzy Rhineheart's father's occupation?
  a. He's a musician.
  b. He's a commercial pilot.
  c. He's an environmentalist.
  d. He's a mercenary pilot.

Q25. How did Lizzy's mother pass away?
  a. In an airplane crash
  b. She drowned
  c. In an avalanche
  d. Spontaneous combustion
  d. In a bizarre gardening accident

The following questions apply to *Where Is Joe Merchant?*

Q26. The following quotation is used to kick off the novel:
  "This book is a pack of lies."
  Which character is quoted?
  a. Rudy Breno
  b. Colonel Adrian Cairo
  c. Blanton Meyercord
  d. Joe Merchant

Q27. The plane was a Grumman Goose JRF-5, powered by two Pratt and Whitney R-985 AN-3 engines, able to generate 450 horsepower each at sea level. What was her name?
  a. *The No-See-Um*
  b. *Daybreak at the Equator*
  c. *The Cosmic Muffin*
  d. *The Hemisphere Dancer*

Q28. Who was known as "The Jet-Ski Killer?
  a. Blanton Meyercord
  b. Trevor Kane
  c. Charlie Fabian
  d. Billy Cruiser

Q29. What was the name of Joe Merchant's most famous hit song?
   a. "Boat Drinks"
   b. "Little Boy Gone"
   c. "Goodbye Cat Girl"
   d. "Twelve Volt Man"

Q30. What were Joe Merchant's famous last words?
   a. "I'll see you later for boat drinks."
   b. The lyrics of his hit song
   c. "You wouldn't want to do that, now would you?"
   d. "It's okay, I do this all of the time."

Q31. What was the trinket that practically everybody was after?
   a. A ruby-encrusted scepter in the shape of a bare-breasted woman
   b. A Spanish dubloon from the treasure of Henri Cristophe
   c. A silver cross laden with diamonds and rubies, rumored to have the power to heal
   d. An extremely rare recording by Joe Merchant

Q32. What was Frank Bama's nickname?
   a. "Ray Ban"
   b. "Comet"
   c. "Brillo"
   d. "Afro"

Q33. Of the following, who is not a character in *Where Is Joe Merchant?* (Choose as many as you think are correct.)
   a. Phil Clark
   b. Desdemona
   c. Root Boy
   d. Guy de la Valdene

Q34. Trevor Kane and her brother Joe Merchant (before he was presumed dead) were wealthy from a family inheritance. What was it that generated all of this money?
   a. Their parents were famous entertainers
   b. Cosmetics

    c. Smuggling

    d. Hemorrhoid ointment

Q35. *Where is Joe Merchant?* consists of fifteen titled chapters that are broken or subdivided into numerous subchapters, each with its own title. Approximately how many numbered subchapters does this novel contain, anyway?

    a. 40

    b. 50

    c. 75

    d. 125

Q36. Counting both chapter titles and subchapter titles, how many of them share titles with Buffett's song catalog? Do not count lyric excerpts, such as "I must confess, I could use some rest" (subchapter no. 37, taken from the lyrics to "Trying to Reason with Hurricane Season"), only actual song titles, or parts of song titles.

    a. 5–7

    b. 9–11

    c. 13–15

    d. 24–27

Q37. With his album projects, Buffett often quotes an excerpt from a novel that he likes on the CD booklet or album jacket in order to set the appropriate mood for the collection of tunes. He does the same thing in his books. What author and book kicks off the text to *Where Is Joe Merchant?*

    a. Bruce Chatwin, *The Song Lines*

    b. Antoine De Saint-Exupery, *Wind, Sand, and Stars*

    c. Mark Twain, *Following the Equator*

    d. Don Blanding, *Floridays*

Q38. Assuming that you've read the hardcover first, then purchased the paperback for a summer re-read, you might be able to answer this one rather easily: Within ten pages, how long is the paperback edition of *Where Is Joe Merchant?*

    a. 350   c. 400

    b. 375   d. 450

Q39. How does Buffett start his own introduction to the novel that follows?
   a. "Once upon a time..."
   b. "His name is Frank Bama, and he flies boats."
   c. "Airplanes are in my blood."
   d. "Where is Joe Merchant?"

Q40. As a summation of sorts, Buffett prints a chorus from one of his own songs on the book's final page. What song is quoted?

ANSWERS

A1. a, d, g, i, and j. a, of course, is the title of his first children's book, written with Savannah Jane, while d, g, i, and j are all included in *Tales From Margaritaville.* f was a trick question, since it was never a song in the first place (0 points for that one, Bub)!

A2. Nope, Snake Bite Key is also a fictional location. On a map, the nearest real-life relative would be Dauphin Island, a long and narrow sandbar that buffers Mobile Bay from the sometimes dangerous storms that rage northward through the Gulf of Mexico during hurricane season.

A3. No again, but the fictional depiction of Heat Wave accurately describes the small Alabama towns of Buffett's youth that hug the Gulf.

A4. Sigh. No again. Look, if it helps, there really is a Denver, Colorado and a Havana, Cuba. As for the others—sorry, Virginia...

A5. c. *Fictional Facts and Factual Fictions* is the subtitle for *Tales From Margaritaville.*

A6. d. *Off to See the Lizard,* besides being the name of an album, is also the title of a story about a high school football team that received some rather bizarre inspiration.

A7. "Write what you know about."

A8.　b. a is the name of the bar on St. Barts that Buffett has been known to frequent, while c is a wonderful hotel on Bourbon Street in New Orleans and d is part of the British Virgin Islands.

A9.　a

A10.　Aurora and Bora Alice (also affectionately known as "Boring Alice") Porter. Take three points if you could only recall their first names, five points if you knew their last name as well.

A11.　The Lizards.

A12　a. Jimmy's previous boat, the ultra-huge Euphoria II, had a state of the art stereo system and was so large that Buffett found it unwieldy to sail, especially when heading into the wind. Regarding electrical power on the Savannah Jane, the sloop contains solar panels which provide just about all of the electricity that the boat needs. If, however, the weather does not cooperate, Buffett could easily find himself at the mercy of prevailing tides until the wind picks up.

A13.　The *Chickamulla*. Buffet mentions this boat in the lyrics to "False Echoes," a tribute to his aging father.

A14.　Freddie Fishstick ("the hottest act on Parrothead Records"). As an aside, Buffett and the Coral Reefers have been known to occasionally appear unannounced at a local club before or after a show, where they would put on a casual performance for the few lucky Parrot Heads who happened to be in attendance. When they do this, they usually operate under the pseudonym of Freddie and the Fishsticks.

A15.　b. Orion is the constellation that appeared on the back of the guitar, along with Albion. Arion (d) is a songwriter from approximately 600 B.C. that Buffett references in his introduction.

A16.　b. Princess Marigold was the daughter of good King Jones.

A17.　a

A18. "Under the heavens and under the sea,
There's a friend I don't know who owns the right key."

On the recorded version from the audio cassette, Savannah Jane duets these lines with the Jolly Mon. By the way, I'm not certain who it is, but unless he is disguising his voice, I don't think it's Savannah Jane's dad who sings the line in tandem with her. Toward the end of the story, this melody is reprised with altered words, taken from the back of the Jolly Mon's magical guitar.

A19. a

A20. Orion

A21. c. All other names are taken from Buffett's own collection of dogs (past and present), as mentioned in his story "Everything in the Woods Wants to Eat a Quail (Including Me)."

A22. c. The *Songbird* (a) is the name of Sky King's airplane (Sky King is one of the characters mentioned in "I Wish I Had a Pencil-Thin Mustache"). *The Savannah Jane* (b) is the name of Buffett's sailboat, while d is the name of his first plane.

A23. b. As for the stupidity of the other choices, give me a break—it's not easy coming up with all of these incorrect answers.

A24. c

A25. c

A26. b. Cairo is the novel's main evil character, a mercenary warrior with ambitions to one day rule his own country and regenerate his missing arm through the magic of the Mayans. Rudy Breno (a) is a cowardly yellow journalist, Blanton Meyercord (c) is a fugitive and close friend of the novel's main character Frank Bama, while Joe Merchant (d) is (or was)…never mind. Read the book.

By the way, for those interested in such things, the hardcover edition of *Where is Joe Merchant?* stayed on the *New York Times* bestseller list for seven months, with three weeks at no. 1.

A27. d. *The No-See-Um* (a) was character Frank Bama's father's plane, *Daybreak at the Equator* (b) is the work-in-progress title of Buffett's next literary, venture, and *Cosmic Muffin* (c) was the name of character Desdemona's boat/rocket ship.

A28   a. Blanton Meyercord, a.k.a. the "Jet-Ski Killer," also went by his nickname of "Ray Ban."

A29. b. The lyrics, as they appear in the novel, are as follows;
        "Little Boy's thinking of the things he's seen
        Scary as the werewolf on a matinee screen
        Little Boy's shrinking like a leprechaun
        Goodbye cruel world, little boy's gone."

A30. b. Although the novel doesn't explicitly state that Joe Merchant was being led to his death, his last scene has him peacefully following the force of the scepter into the sea as he sang the lyrics to "Little Boy Gone."

A31   a

A32. c. "Ray Ban" (a) was the nickname for his friend, Blanton Meyercord, Comet (b) is a household cleanser (sometimes used with Brillo, I suppose) and Afro (d) was the name of Colonel Cairo's green mamba snake.

A33. d is the only correct answer, though I'll bet a lot of you also picked a. Although he never makes a physical appearance, Buffett's old friend and inspiration for "A Pirate Looks at Forty" is mentioned as a plane mechanic who was killed in a Banana Republic coup before the novel caught up with him. Take five points if you picked d only. Otherwise, subtract two points for each incorrect choice (including a).

       For those who are uninformed, Guy de la Valdene is an old Key West friend of Buffett's who was partially responsible for Buffett's early involvement on the soundtrack of a French fishing documentary, as well as a major influence on Buffett's interest in quail hunting.

A34. d

A35. c—76 to be precise.

A36. c. There are precisely thirteen chapter titles that are also song titles. They are 1) "Under the Lone Palm," 2) "That's My Story and I'm Stickin' To It," 3) "Fins to the Left, Fins to the Right," 4) "The Lady I Can't Explain," 5) "Desdemona's Building a Rocket Ship" (yes, the song was written after the book, but it still counts), 6) "Fruitcakes in the Galley, Fruitcakes on the Street," 7) "No Plane on Sunday," 8) "Changing Channels," 9) "Mermaid(s) in the Night," 10) "Happily Ever After (Now and Then)," 11) "Changes in Latitudes," 12) "Where's the Party?" and 13) "Quietly Making Noise." I didn't count "Feeding Frenzy," since it's an album title, not a song title or "Save the Last Dance for Me," since it is written by someone other than Buffett and was only briefly incorporated into one of his own compositions ("Prince of Tides").

A37. b is the correct answer. a is what kicks off *Tales From Margaritaville.*

A38. c. The paperback edition is exactly 399 pages long.

A39 a. D, by the way, is the book's last sentence.

A40. "Happily Ever After (Now and Then)," thus completing the subliminally clever setup of beginning his novel with "Once upon a time…" and ending it with "…happily ever after."

Now, About That Score…

0–100 points—This section is predicated entirely on whether or not you've read the books. The questions were really not so hard this time around, but if you're the type who enjoys the music but ignores the writing, you're predestined to do poorly. Buffett didn't write these books for his health, you know. If you're a fan of the guy, why not read his books? Believe me, it won't kill you and you'll probably have some fun probing Buffett's imagination and entering his make-believe worlds. You might even learn some Buffett-related trivia that could prove useful to you at some other spot in this book.

101–130 points—So you suffer from poor factual retention, huh? I can sympathize with that, especially if you haven't read the books in a while. Or maybe you didn't read all of them and figured that you could bluff your way through the questions that pertained to the books you've skipped. Well, now you know that ploy won't work.

131–200—Any self-respecting Parrot Head knows that Buffett's literature is as important to the artist as his music—lately perhaps even more so. I'm glad to see that you've taken Buffett's desire to get it down on paper seriously, and just as importantly, that you paid attention to what you've read. If you've done well here, then you're obviously going to be a tough nut to crack in the next and final section.

8

The Ultimate Jimmy Buffett Trivia Quiz

OK, so by now, you've had lots of practice and plenty of opportunities to buff up (ouch) on your knowledge. Now, it's time to separate the men from the boys, the tough from the tepid, the slightly unscrewed from the truly lunatic, the...oh, you get the idea. Here's a test that will determine, once and for all, whether or not you really are a Parrot Head, or only a sorry pretender who goes to the concerts to get drunk or get laid (in spite of the invitation proffered in the song title "Let's Get Drunk and Screw," you rarely will get to do both at the same time). If answered honestly, the following questions should determine the degree of your fascination (or as your unsympathetic friends and relatives see it, the hopelessness of your lunacy). Remember, we aren't necessarily searching for the truth, only for the extent of your dedication. Unlike the previous quizzes, there are now *one hundred* questions, and they are worth a total of five points each. That makes the top score...um, let's see, four-eighty, four-ninety...five hundred points! Some questions have semicorrect answers, so partial credit is given when it is appropriate. It is important to keep in mind that the most truthful answer is the best answer.

At the end, why not add up all of your scores from each quiz? Including the introduction, there were eight quizzes worth 200 points each, totaling 1,600 points, and this final quiz worth 500 points. That's a grand total of 2,100 points. Since only God is perfect, we'll consider any score above 2,000 to be a perfect score. For extra credit, you may write a 500 word essay on the topic "What I think I did on my holiday," which must include the full, unedited story of your behavior at a Jimmy Buffett concert, as related to you by friends who claim to have seen the whole thing before you passed out. Send the essay along with your test results to the publisher of this book (honesty counts here, folks) who will then forward them to me. If your score makes the grade (and if you include return postage), I will send you an official Master's Degree in Jimmy Buffett-ology. Good luck.

THE QUIZ—This time, it's for real...

Q1. How many albums has Jimmy Buffett released (plus or minus three) from the start of his career until the end of 1996? Note: Count domestic releases of new material and live albums only (for example, *Before the Beach* and *Songs You Know by Heart* don't count).

    a. 10

    b. 15

    c. 20

    d. 25

    e. 250

Q2. Oh yeah, wise guy? Name 'em. (Give yourself 1 point for every 5 titles you can name that appear in the answer section. Maximum score 5 points.)

Q3. From the below list, eliminate the choice that is least likely to be cited (at least not yet, anyway) as an influence on the young Jimmy Buffett.

    a. Spike Jones

    b. Mark Twain

    c. Robert Louis Stevenson

    d. Minnie Pearl

    e. *Adventures In Paradise*

    f. *Sing Along With Mitch* (Miller)

Q4. Jimmy Buffett, along with comedian Bill Murray, Yankees part-owner Marvin Goldklang, and president and active owner Mike Veeck (son of baseball's well-known eccentric Bill Veeck—rhymes with "wreck") are the coowners of one of baseball's most successful minor-league teams, the St. Paul (Minnesota) Saints. Which one of the following promotional stunts was *not* utilized by the team to enhance the draw at the gate?

    a. They hired a pig with an eye patch for a mascot

    b. They hired someone to dress as a nun and give back massages to the fans in the stands

    c. Disco Demolition Night (a fiasco that led to a forfeit)

    d. Parrot Head Night, a chance for Buffett fans to get some other use from their ridiculous headgear

   e. They built a sandbox "beach" on top of the home-team dugout, where fans can lounge with parasols

   f. *Wizard of Oz* Night, where people were requested to dress as characters from the movie

   g. Silent Night, where the audience was instructed to perform mime

Q5. For a good time, call
   a. 504-592-2565
   b. 504-555-1212
   c. 800-COCOTEL
   d. 800-432-JOIN

Q6. For this section, match the name of the tour with the year that it took place.

a. The Chameleon Caravan Tour	1.	1993
b. Recession Recess	2.	1992
c. Domino College	3	1995
d. Jimmy's Jump Up Tour	4.	1990
e. The Outpost (Margaritaville Clipper) Tour	5.	1991
f. The Living Room Tour	6.	1989
g. The Banana Wind Tour	7.	1996

Q7. What was the color, year, make, and model of "God's Own Truck"?
   a. A light green '59 Ford pickup
   b. An aquamarine '53 Chevy pickup
   c. A green '74 Ford Bronco
   d. An aqua '57 Chevy pickup

Q8. If you went to Margaritaville in New Orleans, which of the items below could you actually order off of the menu (choose as many as you think are correct)?
   a. The Somewhere Over China Chicken Salad
   b. The Cheeseburger In Paradise
   c. The Livingston's Texas Ribeye
   d. Jambalaya

Q9. According to *Forbes* magazine, who could claim the highest income for (fiscal year) 1994?
   a. Bill Gates
   b. Steve Forbes
   c. Warren Buffett
   d. Jimmy Buffett and Don Henley combined have more money than any of those guys
   e. Who's Warren Buffett, Bill Gates, or Steve Forbes?

Q10. Who was the highest-paid entertainer in the world, based on *Forbes* magazine's (founded by Steve's father, Malcolm, by the way) gross estimated income for 1994–95?
   a. O. J. Simpson
   b. Barry Manilow
   c. Ross Perot
   d. Jimmy Buffett
   e. Warren Buffett
   f. Oprah Winfrey
   g. Stephen Spielberg

OK, enough with the easy multiple choice questions. For the next few, you must provide the answer.

Q11. What do David Bowie, Susan Sontag, and Jimmy Buffett all have in common?

Q12. To answer this question properly, you not only need to be familiar with the original inner sleeve that was provided with the *Changes in Latitudes, Changes in Attitudes* album, but you must also have a keen eye for detail and a taste for the absurd. Ready? On this inner sleeve, the album's lyrics are hand-lettered, along with a few credits and a few notes. I could find no credit for the person who handled the lettering, but it's a safe bet that it was not done by Jimmy. I can say this with confidence because not only are few of the lyrics messed up, but some of the misspellings are so ridiculous as to be funny. For example, the album photos are credited to Tom Corchoran (instead of Corcoran) and—get this—Jane Slalsudl. Slalsudl? It sounds like a cryptoquote, for God's sake. I would think Jimmy would know the proper way to spell his future wife's maiden name, no? Anyway, at the bottom, Jimmy penned a quick note thanking a few people and then signs off, saying "aboard the…" Aboard the what? That's the question.

Q13. On the inner gate-fold of the *Volcano* album is a poem from a collection of work that was written in 1941 called *Floridays* (that's right, just like the later Buffett album), credited to Don Blanding. What is the name of the poem?

Q14. What song has Jimmy blowing a few holes in his freezer?

Q15. Here's a toughie. Following are the instrumental credits as they appear on the back cover of *which album?* Larry Fiel—guitar, Rick Fiel—bass guitar, Paul Tabot—drums, Bergen White—trombone, Bobby Thompson—banjo, Randy Goodrum and Buzz Cason—keyboards.

Q16. The following lyrics are excerpted from a Buffett-penned theme song for an early '70s failed TV pilot. Name the show it was intended for.

> "Life's too complicated, it's too complex
> Bounce from town to town like rubber checks
> Didn't know at the time I'd pay double for the crime
> Not to mention a serious problem with the opposite sex"

Q17. This is for hardcore fans only: The song "Tin Cup Chalice" from *A1A* has the lyric "fill it up with good, red wine." In its demo form, though, Buffett apparently hadn't yet developed such fine tastes. What was the original content of the chalice?

Q18. How many top 10 singles has Jimmy Buffett recorded?

Q19. How many top 40 singles has Jimmy Buffett recorded ($+/-$ 1 is acceptable)?

Q20. How many top 100 singles ($+/-$ 2 is acceptable)?

Q21. In what year did JB have his last top 100 single ($+/-$ 1 year is OK)?

Q22. Jimmy Buffett sings background vocals on one Eagles song. Name the song (2 points), the album it appears on (1 pt), and the fictitious name for the vocal group he was a part of (2 more points).

Q23. In the *Esquire* sportsman article "Everything in the Woods Wants to Eat a Quail (Including Me)," Buffett mentions four of his dogs (living and deceased). Can you name all four?

Q24. In 1987, the Neville Brothers released an album that featured two Buffett-Utley-Jennings compositions. What was the name of the album?

Q25. While we're on the subject of other people's albums, Buffett cowrote a song with James Taylor called "Sugar Trade" that appeared on Taylor's 1987 album release. Name the album that this song appeared on.

And now, for a little bit of mercy, back to multiple choice.

Q26. Who is the accredited backing vocal group on "Treat Her Like a Lady," from *Volcano?*
   a. Whipple and the Charmin Squeezers
   b. Those Dirty Rings
   c. The Reefer-ettes
   d. The Embarrassing Stains
   e. The Del-Vikings
   f. The Five Satins

Q27. In the 10/4/79 *Rolling Stone* article, Buffett is overheard demanding that his manager Irving Azoff send a couple of things down to Montserrat. One was money. What was the other?
   a. Even more money
   b. 12 tennis balls
   c. 12 Ping-Pong balls
   d. 12 golf balls
   e. 12 bowling balls
   f. 12 baseballs

Q28. The song "Fins" has in it the line "...postcards from the road." More than likely, this was a conscious reference to a friend's recently published autobiography. Whose?

    a. Elizabeth Ashley

    b. Margot Kidder

    c. Hunter Thompson

    d. Carrie Fisher

Q29. In the October 4, 1979 *Rolling Stone* cover story, Buffett was supposed to meet Chet Flippo at an open-air bar called Le Select (by the way, he mentions this bar on "A Sailor's Christmas"), on the island of St. Barts. In later years, this bar became a restaurant, and for awhile, the name of the establishment was changed. To what?

    a. The Margaritaville Cafe

    b. Captain Tony's

    c. Chez Jimmy

    d. Cheeseburger In Paradise

Q30. What activist organization has its logo appear on the inside jacket of *Coconut Telegraph?*

    a. Amnesty International

    b. Greenpeace

    c. Save the Manatees

    d. The Audobon Society

    e. Save the Whales

Q31. Finish the following credit: "Strings and horns 'On a Slow Boat to China' deranged by"...

    a. Michael Utley

    b. Norbert Putnam

    c. Freddie Fishstick

    d. Jimmy Buffett

Q32. What English star eventually bought Jerry Jeff Walker's Packard (the "Flying Lady" was her nickname), the car that is credited with carrying Buffett to Key West for the first time and featured prominently on the cover of *Before the Beach?*

    a. Dave Edmunds

    b. Ian Anderson

   c. Rick Wakeman
   d. Jon Anderson

Q33. On what Jimmy Buffett album does Michael Utley make his debut appearance?
   a. *A White Sport Coat and a Pink Crustacean*
   b. *Volcano*
   c. *Somewhere Over China*
   d. *Riddles in the Sand*

Q34. Match the song title with the movie that it appeared in. Note that there are six song titles and seven movies. This is not an accident. By the way, taken as a whole, you might care to note from the below song titles that Buffett is quite talented when it comes to writing on demand for a particular film's topic...

   a. *FM*
   b. *Summer Rental*
   c. *Arachnophobia*
   d. *Coast to Coast*
   e. *Fast Times at Ridgemont High*
   f. *Urban Cowboy*
   g. *Rancho Deluxe*

   1. "Don't Bug Me"
   2. "Turning Around"
   3. "Livingston Saturday Night"
   4. "I Don't Know"
   5. "Hello Texas"
   6. "Survive"

Q35. When did Corona Beer begin to sponsor Jimmy Buffett concerts (or when did JB start to sponsor Corona Beer, depending on your point of view)?
   a. 1981
   b. 1982
   c. 1984
   d. 1986

Q36. In their review for a certain album, *Rolling Stone* magazine referred to Jimmy Buffett as "a water-logged James Taylor impersonator." Which album were they discussing?
   a. *Hot Water*
   b. *Coconut Telegraph*
   c. *Off to See the Lizard*
   d. *Fruitcakes*

Q37. What was the name of the sailboat that Rip Torn, John
     Candy, and his (film) family were repairing while the
     soundtrack played the Buffett/Utley/Jennings composition
     "Turning Around?"
     a. *The Eudaurm*
     b. *The Euphoria*
     c. *The Barnacle*
     d. *The Will O' the Wisp*
     e. *The Escapade*

Q38. In the liner notes of *Boats, Beaches, Bars, and Ballads*,
     what song does Buffet claim to be the first that he wrote
     upon arriving in Key West?
     a. "I Have Found Me a Home"
     b. "Nautical Wheelers"
     c. "He Went to Paris"
     d. "Tin Cup Chalice"

Q39. Which of the following is credited for singing the backup
     vocals on "Elvis Imitators?"
     a. Fingers Taylor, Josh Leo, Harry Dailey, and Vince
        Melamed, a.k.a the Duck Bills
     b. The Jordanaires
     c. The Statler Brothers
     d. The Oak Ridge Boys

Q40. What is the name of the main character in "Don't Stop the
     Carnival"?
     a. Malcolm Pepperman
     b. Norman Paperman
     c. Howie Silverman
     d. Max Bialystock

And now, a few more questions without multiple choices...

Q41. In 1985, the song "Christmas in the Caribbean" appeared
     on an MCA collection of country-styled Christmas songs.
     What was the name of this collection?

Q42. As he tells the story on "You Had to Be There," what was
     the name of the drive-in theater where Jimmy "commits a
     little mortal sin?"

Q43. Who produced *The Parakeet Album?*

Q44. Herman Wouk was, of course, responsible for the 1965 novel, *Don't Stop the Carnival.* Which of the following works were also written by Wouk?
   a. *The Caine Mutiny*
   b. *War and Remembrance*
   c. *The Winds of War*
   d. *Youngblood Hawke*
   e. *Marjorie Morningstar*

Q45. Which of the following titles does *not* have an accompanying video?
   a. "Fruitcakes"
   b. "Another Saturday Night"
   c. "School Boy Heart"
   d. "One Particular Harbor"
   e. "Jamaica Farewell"
   f. "La Vie Dansante"
   g. "Take Another Road"
   h. "Who's the Blond Stranger"
   i. "Homemade Music"
   j. "Gypsies in the Palace"

Ready to scream "Uncle"? Here's the final five for the first half, mercifully in the form of multiple choice:

Q46. Amy Lee is Jimmy's sax player and like most of the Coral Reefers, is also an occasional writing partner. Which of the below song titles is she credited with coauthoring (here's a hint: only one applies)?
   a. "Fruitcakes"
   b. "Everybody's Got a Cousin in Miami"
   c. "Quietly Making Noise"
   d. "Love in the Library"

Q47. Since I brought up the subject of Buffett's bandmembers, I think I should note that besides his generosity with writing credits, Buffett is also often kind enough to let some of the Coral Reefers perform a song or two during the course of a show. Recently, background singer Nadirah

Shakoor occasionally sings a song that appeared on the
Utley/Greenidge album *Club Trini*, called "Love is Made of
This." What band was Shakoor a member of before her
tenure with the Coral Reefers?

   a. Arrested Development
   b. Digable Planets
   c. Planet Soul
   d. TLC

Q48. Which of the following artists have *not* appeared on Frank
Sinatra's *Duets* album series (Jimmy Buffett appears on
Volume II)?

   a. Bono Vox
   b. Willie Nelson
   c. Aaron Neville
   d. Chrissie Hynde
   e. Kenny G

Q49. Which of the following song titles are a part of *Don't Stop
the Carnival* (at least in its present incarnation)?

   a. "The Key to My Man"
   b. "A Thousand Steps to Nowhere"
   c. "I'm Gonna Wash That Man Right Out of My Hair"
   d. "Kinja Rules"
   e. "Who Are We Trying to Fool"
   f. "Some Enchanted Evening"

Q50. In his early Key West days, Buffett had a beachfront
apartment (the one he leased to Hunter Thompson) that
was located directly next door to a bar. What was the
name of the bar?

   a. Louie's Backyard
   b. The Full Moon Saloon
   c. The Chart Room
   d. The Old Anchor Inn
   e. The Margaritaville Cafe

Okay, you're halfway through. If you want to pause here, get up
and stretch, perhaps freshen up your drink, go right ahead.
Then, get back to work.

Q51. Back to the earlier years for a few questions. *A1A* yielded only one single, and it sold poorly. What was it?
   a. "Makin' Music For Money"
   b. "Saxophones"
   c. "Life is Just a Tire Swing"
   d. "A Pirate Looks at Forty"

Q52. Okay maybe that was too easy. Just to make things a bit more interesting, can you pick the B-side of that single release?
   a. "Dallas"
   b. "Presents to Send You"
   c. "Door Number Three"
   d. "Stories We Could Tell"

I'm having too much fun coming up with trivia from what I consider to be one of Buffett's best albums, so here's a few more *A1A*-related questions;

Q53. Who wrote "Stories We Could Tell"?
   a. John Sebastian
   b. Alex Harvey
   c. Roger Bartlett
   d. Jimmy Buffett
   e. Fingers Taylor
   f. Steve Goodman

Q54. Who wrote "Makin' Music for Money"?
   a. John Sebastian
   b. Alex Harvey
   c. Roger Bartlett
   d. Jimmy Buffett
   e. Fingers Taylor
   f. Steve Goodman

Q55. Who wrote "Dallas"?
   a. John Sebastian
   b. Alex Harvey
   c. Roger Bartlett
   d. Jimmy Buffett
   e. Fingers Taylor
   f. Steve Goodman

Q56. Who wrote "Life Is Just a Tire Swing"?
    a. John Sebastian
    b. Alex Harvey
    c. Roger Bartlett
    d. Jimmy Buffett
    e. Fingers Taylor
    f. Steve Goodman

Q57. Who wrote "Big Rig" (yes, I know it's not from *A1A*)?
    a. John Sebastian
    b. Alex Harvey
    c. Roger Bartlett
    d. Jimmy Buffett
    e. Fingers Taylor
    f. Steve Goodman

Here's a few more lyrical phrases that I want you to finish, with a clue; they're all from the *A1A* album:

Q58. "They're ugly and square and they don't belong here…"

Q59. "I'd never been west of New Orleans…"

Q60. "Kiss me I'm a baker…"

Q61. Okay, enough of that. What album features the song "Wonder Why You Ever Go Home"?

Q62. Buffett's marriage to Jane Slagsvol took place in
    a. Redstone, Colorado
    b. Aspen, Colorado
    c. Miami, Florida
    d. Key West, Florida

Q63. In the liner notes to the *Havana Daydreamin'* album, Buffett mentions that "the white suit and parakeet are still waiting for that future date when we sail away to Martinique." What's he referring to (can I make a bad pun and say "Reefer-ing to"?
    a. The lyrics to the song "Havana Daydreamin'"
    b. The movie *Key Largo*
    c. The movie *Casablanca*
    d. The lyrics to "Migration"

Q64. According to the lyrics of "Changes in Latitudes, Changes in Attitudes," what does Jimmy think about when he's high on red wine?

Q65. Can you name three songs that originally appeared on the early Barnaby albums that Buffett saw fit to re-record and release on ABC?

Q66. In "Big Rig," what show is the narrator stuck watching on his hotel television instead of being home?
   a. Johnny Carson
   b. Mike Douglas
   c. Tom Snyder
   d. Merv Griffin

And now for a few questions that concern themselves with Buffett's first live album, a double-album gatefold package from 1978. Before we get started, though, maybe you ought go pull the album out of your collection and scrape all of the embarrassing marijuana residue from the inner crease of the gatefold cover. (Remember when everybody used to "clean their pot" on the inside of album jackets like this one, or am I incriminating myself here?) I bought a used copy of *You Had to Be There* just recently and sure enough, there on the inside crease was a visible amount of green powder still lingering.

My, how times have changed.

For this section, I'm going to quote a few "alternate" lyrics. For five points, you provide the song title that I am quoting (remember, these are the lyrics as they appear on the live album, not the studio track). Then, finish the phrase for another 5 points.

Q67 and Q68. "God, I still feel pain, I wish I had some cocaine...."

Q69 and Q70. "This cast is no blast but it's comin' off fast...."

Q71 and Q72. "They consume mass quantities of fiberglass...."

Okay, so much for the live album, let's move on.

Fill in the blank to the following lyrics (5 points) and the song that is being quoted (5 points):

Q73 and Q74. "She's _____ from the Chart Room."

Q75 and Q76. "Stashed his trash in _____, bought a good suit of clothes."

Q77 and Q78. "Making points with the _____ climbing over Long Island Sound."

Okay, then, no more of these sneaky ten-point questions disguised as five-pointers. Back to standard multiple choice.

Q79. Which of the following songs could be said to most resemble the general idea behind the plot of Herman Wouk's *Don't Stop the Carnival?*
   a. "Boat Drinks"
   b. "The Weather is Here, Wish You Were Beautiful"
   c. "Steamer"
   d. "Who's the Blond Stranger"

Q80. On *Feeding Frenzy*, Buffett mentions the names of a few of his opportunistic house-sitters. One is Snake. Who are the other gypsies in the palace?
   a. Johnny D.
   b. The Everlasting Moonie
   c. Bubba
   d. Dare T.
   e. Kyle E.

Q81. Okay, speaking of live albums, there are sixteen tracks listed for Buffett's second collection of live material, *Feeding Frenzy*. How many of these sixteen tracks appeared previously on his first live collection, *You Had to Be There?*
   a. 2
   b. 4
   c. 6
   d. 8

Q82. Fine, but let's not forget that this is supposed to be the *tough* quiz. Assuming that you knew the answer to the previous question, with this query I'm expecting you to name the songs that are duplicated on the two live albums.

To be kind and to prevent confusion, I'll start you off. "Why Don't We Get Drunk" appears on both (but the title is changed on *Feeding Frenzy* to "A Love Song From a Different Point of View"). That's one. You name the rest.

Q83. What song and album combination starts with the sound of a street parade?
   a. "Everybody's Got a Cousin in Miami"/*Fruitcakes*
   b. "Barometer Soup"/*Barometer Soup*
   c. "Christmas Island"/*Christmas Island*
   d. "Only Time Will Tell"/*Banana Wind*
   e. "You'll Never Work in Dis Bidness Again"/*Feeding Frenzy*

Q84. Every now and then, Buffett is known to throw in a reference to his time spent as an altar boy. What Buffett recording features an excerpt from the old-fashioned Latin days of Roman Catholicism in the lyrics?
   a. "Pascagoula Run"
   b. "Life is Just a Tire Swing"
   c. "Migration"
   d. "Fruitcakes"

Q85. What Buffett song has the following rhyme scheme: rolls/souls, dance/France, stars/cigars, skill/deal?

Q86. Some rhymes are so improbable that you can't help but be impressed by the writer's intuition. What Buffett song is clever enough to rhyme "stairs" with "Flaubert"?

Q87. Buffett's character Desdemona, from *Where Is Joe Merchant?*, also crops up as a character in two of Buffett's songs. Name both of them.

Q88. What song clocks in as Buffett's longest?
   a. "Fruitcakes"
   b. "Everybody's Got a Cousin in Miami"
   c. "Desdemona's Building a Rocket Ship"
   d. "God's Own Drunk"
   e. "Creola"
   f. "False Echoes"

Q89. Fingers Taylor started releasing his solo projects some time in the mid-eighties. His first record was called *Harpoon Man.* Can you name the band that backs him up on this record?

Q90. Christmas is mostly a time for tradition and Buffett's Christmas album contains a number of seasonal classics. There are, however, a few original songs thrown into the mix that he surely hopes will become a part of the Parrot Heads' Christmas tradition. How many songs on *Christmas Island* are originals, and can you name them all?

Q92. In the lyrics to "False Echoes," Buffett recounts the special events that took place on his father's first birthday, and mentions the date. What, then, is his father's birthday?
  a. 11/25/1920
  b. 12/25/1920
  c. 11/25/1921
  d. 12/25/1921

Q93. Match the product with the song where it appears in the lyrics:

  a. Bryl Creem   1. "Life is Just a Tire Swing"
  b. Hush Puppies   2. "Come Monday"
  c. Tony Lama's   3. "It's Midnight and I'm Not
  d. Darvon   Famous Yet"
  e. RCA Victrola   4. "Pencil Thin Mustache"
  f. Gucci shoes   5. "My Head Hurts, My Feet
                            Stink and I Don't Love Jesus"
                         6. "Livingston Saturday Night"

Q94. Match the real-life character with the song that mentions him or her.

  a. Oscar Wilde   1. "Fruitcakes"
  b. Stanley   2. "Six String Music"
     Kubrick   3. "Quietly Making Noise"
  c. Sir Francis and   4. "Vampires, Mummies and the
     Elizabeth   Holy Ghost"
  d. Beethoven   5. "Love in the Library"
  e. Stephen King

Q95. Match the fictional character with the song that mentions them.

a. Jesus	1. "Who's the Blond Stranger"
b. Joe Bones	2. "Coconut Telegraph"
c. Melissa and Ricardo	3. "Havana Daydreamin'"
d. Lola	4. "That's My Story and I'm Stickin' To It"
e. Sister Mary Mojo	5. "My Head Hurts, My Feet Stink and I Don't Love Jesus"

Q96. Match the author with the song that mentions him (or her).

a. Louis L'Amour	1. "If It All Falls Down"
b. James Jones	2. "Who's the Blond Stranger"
c. John D. MacDonald	3. "That's What Livin' Is to Me"
d. Faulkner	4. "Incommunicado"
e. James Joyce and Agatha Christie	5. "If I Could Only Get It on Paper"
f. Mark Twain	6. "Sending the Old Man Home"

Q97. For his 1997 summer tour, Buffett comically altered the lyrics of "Why Don't We Get Drunk and Screw" to something that is considerably more family-ready. What is the title of this revamped sing-along?

Q98. Name both the A-side and the B-side of Buffett's very first single, and no, I'm not talking about "The Christian?" I'm going even further back, to the single he recorded prior to his Barnaby days.

Q99. Now for one that's even older. Name the one song recorded and released by Buffett that was published before his birthdate (Note: Only songs that appear on actual Jimmy Buffett albums count for this one).

Q100. For the final question, I've decided to forego multiple choice. For the last chance that you have to prove that you're a Parrot Head, tell me the name of the father/son duo that adds emotional as well as timbral resonances to Buffett's song about the passing of generations, *Banana Wind*'s "False Echoes."

That's it. Pens down. I said PENS DOWN! It looks like an awful lot of you are going to have to go to summer school, doesn't it? That's okay, though, because the good news is that summer school of the Buffett variety simply means going to a concert or two, so don't look so glum. All in all, though, I bet you did awfully, didn't you? Harder than you thought, eh? Well, why are you blaming me?! You mean you thought I was a little bit too tough and spent too much time on topics that were only peripherally related? Well, from what I've seen and heard, most Parrot Heads latch on to anything that becomes associated with Buffett, so I don't think that I was being unfair at all. Still, though, I'd hate to see you go away mad.

Oh, all right already. You need a chance at some extra credit? Okay, I'll give you one last chance. And THAT'S IT!! After that, you're on your own. Choose either of the following two questions for a chance at a few extra points:

Extra Credit No. 1—For ten free points: According to the *Coconut Telegraph*, what is Jimmy Buffett's sports jersey number?

Extra Credit No. 2—For TWENTY free points: For years now, Jimmy seems to consider eight songs to be essential to his live show. Name all eight songs. You may make ten selections to match the eight that appear in my list.

Points are ALL OR NOTHING (i.e., if you choose No. 2, you must name all eight that appear in the answer section, and keep in mind that you might think I'm wrong! You may choose EITHER No. 1 or No. 2, but NOT BOTH!). Willing to risk it?

Good luck.

THE ANSWERS

A1.   a, b, or c. Sorry, but no. 0 points
d. There are twenty-five, if you count *Boats, Beaches, Bars, and Ballads* and the soundtrack album *Rancho Deluxe*. Even if you didn't count these two, that'd be

twenty-three, still making this the closest answer. Take 5 points

e. If you picked e, then you'll probably *eventually* be right, so take 2 points.

A2. 1. *Down To Earth*
2. *High Cumberland Jubilee*
3. *A White Sport Coat and a Pink Crustacean*
4. *Living and Dying in ³/₄ Time*
5. *A-1-A*
6. *"Rancho Deluxe" Soundtrack*
7. *Havana Daydreamin'*
8. *Changes in Latitudes, Changes in Attitudes*
9. *Son of a Son of a Sailor*
10. *You Had to Be There* (Live, Double)
11. *Volcano*
12. *Coconut Telegraph*
13. *Somewhere Over China*
14. *One Particular Harbor*
15. *Riddles in the Sand*
16. *Last Mango in Paris*
17. *Floridays*
18. *Hot Water*
19. *Off to See the Lizard*
20. *Feeding Frenzy* (Live)
21. *Boats, Beaches, Bars, and Ballads*
22. *Fruitcakes*
23. *Barometer Soup*
24. *Banana Wind*
25. *Christmas Island* (a holiday album)

Remember, ONE POINT for every 5 correct answers.

A3. a. Spike Jones used to tour the Southern circuit, bringing his aural mayhem on the road, and Jimmy claims to have been highly impressed by his shows when he was a kid. 0 points

b. Mark Twain was and still is a huge influence on JB, not just for his humor and his wonderful characterizations, but for the inspiration he provides as a master writer of American fiction. 0 points. In fact, subtract a point if you didn't know this. − 1 point, bub.

c. Robert Louis Stevenson wrote *Treasure Island*. Need I say more? 0 points

d. To the best of my knowledge, Jimmy has yet to perform with a price tag dangling from his cap. His humor might occasionally be a bit *Hee-Haw*-ish, but that's mostly just a coincidence. 5 points

e. *Adventures in Paradise* was an ABC-TV show that ran for four seasons in the early sixties. It featured the ongoing saga of a schooner captain in the South Pacific, and his adventures with beautiful women and exotic locales. JB claims that the show "made me want to get the hell away from Mobile." 0 points

f. Mitch Miller was the head of Artists and Repertoire (A&R) at Columbia Records in the late fifties-early sixties. He was known for having a boundless hatred for anything resembling rock and roll, but he was much better known for his television show and record albums featuring stale sing-along versions of crusty standards. Young Jimmy ate it up when he was a kid. 0 points

A4. Here is a case where the least likely choice is also the only correct choice. The only event that was not arranged to promote the Saints was Parrot Head Day. If you said so, give yourself 5 points!

A5. a. 504-592-2565 is the telephone number to Jimmy Buffett's Margaritaville, on Decatur Street in New Orleans. 5 points if you picked this

b. This is the number for New Orleans information. 0 points

c. This is the number you'd dial if you wanted to order Buffett-related merchandise through his newsletter, the *Coconut Telegraph*. You can buy stuff here, but you can't arrange a party (unless you're calling about one of their prearranged vacations), so take a point for recognizing the Buffett connection.

d. It may not be for a good time, but it is certainly for a good cause. This is the number to dial if you seek information about or wish to contribute to the Save the Manatees Club, cochaired by Jimmy Buffett. Since we're talking about charity, take two points.

A6. a-1, b-2, c-3, d-4, e-5, f-6, g-7

Take five points for all matches correct. Otherwise, add one for each correct match and subtract one for each incorrect match.

A7. b. Even back then, it was one old sucker. Through the rust and spray paint, you could barely make out the name of the previous owner that was lettered on the driver's door—Monroe County Glass and Mirror.

A8. a, b, c, and d are all correct! Give yourself one point for each one you picked. If you picked all four, then give yourself 5 points.

A9. a. Although he is usually rated as the richest man in the world, it appears as though the founder of Microsoft had taken a temporary back seat to another entrepreneur and savvy investor in 1994. Perhaps it was due to his front-loaded investment in Windows '95. Read on. (Take 2 points—horseshoe rules)

b. Steve Forbes may have a connection to the magazine that publishes these things, may have been blessed with a rich dad, and he might have lofty political aspirations as well, but he wasn't the highest earner in '94. 0 points

c. Because of his remarkable investing acumen and God only knows what else it takes to achieve such status, Warren Buffett was deemed the most successful investor of 1994. What does that have to do with Jimmy Buffett? Not much more than a shared surname and a supposed distant relation, but right is right, so if you guessed this, then give yourself 5 points.

d. Wishful thinking. These guys might be extravagantly wealthy by your or my standards, but in comparison to the above three, they're a pair of pikers. Give yourself 2 points,

though, just for being so faithful (not to mention incredi-
bly wrong).

e. Good answer. If you picked this, then I can only assume
that you are such an out-of-your-head Buffett fanatic that
you don't have time for current events (or an interest
either, for that matter). Give yourself 2 points, then ask
yourself the following questions: a) Who is Al Gore? b)
Who is Madonna? c) Who is Pope John Paul? If you didn't
get any of these either, then give yourself a full two
hundred and fifty points and get back to your CD collection. Sorry if we've disturbed you.

A10. a. This would only be possible if you have a thoroughly
deranged or loose definition of the word "entertainer." 0
points

b. This would only be possible if you have a thoroughly
deranged or loose definition of the word "entertainer." 0
points

c. This would only be possible if you have a thoroughly
deranged or loose definition of the word "entertainer," but
I think ol' Ross deserves partial credit for making all of
those cool charts that he flashes us on TV. Take 1 point,
even though I don't have the foggiest notion of how much
money he makes.

d. Wishful thinking again, I'm afraid. Jimmy Buffett did
make the list though, at no. 36, with $26 million. He was
listed in back of other such notable (and lucre-dipped)
musical artists as Aerosmith (no. 32 at $30 million), Boyz
II Men (no. 31 at $31 mil), Billy Joel (no. 26 at $33 mil),
Elton John (no. 24 at $35 mil), Garth Brooks (no. 19 at $40
big ones), The Grateful Dead (no. 16 at $42 mil), Barbra
Streisand (what do expect when you charge 250 bucks for
one measly ticket?—no. 9 at $63 mil), Michael Jackson
(no. 8 at $67 mil), Pink Floyd (no. 7 at $70 mil), The Eagles
(Hell Freezes Over indeed, but what do you expect when
you charge…no. 5 at $95 mil), The Rolling Stones (the
longest running act in the business, at the no. 4 position
with $121 million), The Beatles (!!! I thought these guys

broke up, yet here they are twenty five years later, and they're still statistically kicking the Rolling Stones' butt, at no. 3 with $130 million). Nevertheless, you are apparently so enamored with Jimmy Buffett's abilities to earn and entertain that you deserve the benefit of the doubt, if only for remaining faithful to your favorite artist (and relevant to the topic of this book). 3 points

e. This would only be possible if you have a thoroughly deranged or loose definition of the word "entertainer." 0 points.

f. In a perfect world, this would only be possible if... but it's not a perfect world and Oprah locked in at second place with a cool $146 million in estimated earnings. Like horseshoes, though, close counts. Give yourself a point.

g. Right is right. Mr. Spielberg made so much money that he practically doubled his nearest contender (see Oprah, above), earning an estimated $285 million in 1994–95. 5 points. If it will make you feel any better, you might better be able to put this whole ridiculous exercise into perspective when I tell you that Barney (yep, *that* Barney, the pudgy, purple dinosaur) earned 40 million bucks, placing him at no. 17, 19 positions higher than Jimmy Buffett. See, I told you it wasn't a perfect world.

A11. All had their names appear on the cover of the *Rolling Stone* issue that featured Jimmy's photo and feature article. Other than that they don't have too much in common at all. If you guessed that, then take five points. If you are obsessive enough to know the date of the issue (October 4, 1979) give yourself an extra two points and next time, write your own damn book.

A12. "Aboard the *Eudaurm*—Coconut Grove, Florida, December 20, 1976." Now, I don't need to be a brain surgeon to figure that Jimmy was not writing us from a boat called "*THE EUDAURM.*" I mean, who in their right mind would give a boat an unpronounceable name like that? It could be a body part on an insect, or maybe part of the esophagus, but not a boat. If you look at the word long enough, you'll recognize that the word euphoria could be mistaken for EUDAURM if it was scribbled sloppily enough. Apparently, Jimmy tossed off a quick hand-written note, and the letters were misinterpreted, but c'mon, guys, who's your proofreader?

A13. "Mystery South of Us."

A14. "Boat Drinks," from *Volcano*. In an attempt to convey a bad case of wintry cabin fever, the song's character decides to take his frost-free frustration out on his icebox. Buffett claims that he actually did this during a Nashville frost.

A15. These are the instrumental credits for *High Cumberland Jubilee*, the infamous "lost" album that was not officially released until considerably after it was finished. On the cover of the original album, Buffett can be seen sitting by a fireplace with friends, playing the mandolin.

A16. The show was called *Johnny Bago*.

A17. On a demo version that I stumbled across, Buffett sings about filling his chalice with "apple wine."

A18. "Margaritaville" was Jimmy's only top ten single. It reached No. 8.

A19. Add "Come Monday" (no. 30), "Changes in Latitudes, Changes in Attitudes" (no. 37), "Cheeseburger in Paradise" (no. 32), and "Fins" (no. 35) to "Margaritaville." That's a total of five.

A20. There are five more to add to the above list of five. They are "Livingston Saturday Night" (no. 52), "Manana" (no. 84), "*Volcano*" (no. 66), "Survive" (no. 77), and "It's My Job" (no. 57). That's a total of ten.

A21. 1981, with "It's My Job." Obviously, Jimmy's fan base isn't too interested in spinning the old 45's. I'd say that they are primarily concerned with his live performances, with albums making adequate souvenirs until the next time he rolls around. Singles just don't cut it for the Parrot Heads, though.

A22. Jimmy sings as part of the background chorus for the painfully unfunny "The Greeks Don't Want No Freaks," from *The Long Run*. The vocal group was credited as "The Monstertones, featuring J. Buffett."

A23. Buffett's hunting dogs, as they appear in the article, are (1) Summer, his current springer spaniel, (2) Biff, his german short-hair pointer, (3) Cheeseburger, his golden retriever who has been "retired" and (4) Spring, his prized springer spaniel who has since passed away. Take five points if you got all of them or one point for each. If you were able to name others, they don't count count here since the question applies only to those mentioned in the *Esquire* article (sorry about that).

A24. *Uptown.*

A25. *Dad Loves His Work.*

A26. d. They call themselves the Embarrassing Stains, and I don't think that I want to know why…James Taylor, his brothers Alex and Hugh, Deborah McColl, and Dave Loggins (who is also Buffett's songwriting collaborator here—remember him from "Please Come to Boston"? He's also Kenny's cousin) are the group members.

A27. c. Buffett wanted to play Ping Pong, but there were no Ping-Pong balls to be found on the island of Montserrat.

A28. d. Carrie Fischer would eventually release her own book, similarly titled *Postcards From the Edge.*

A29. d

A30. b

A31. a

A32. c. Rick Wakeman is the keyboardist best known for his work as a member of the art-rock group Yes. After purchasing the car, he had it flown to England.

A33. a. Many fans don't realize it, but Michael Utley was right there on Buffett's very first studio album for ABC Records.

A34. a-3, b-2, c-1, d-6, e-4, f-5, g-3. Take 5 points only if you got everything right. Otherwise, take 1 point for each correct match.

A35. c

A36. c. *Rolling Stone* made their rather scathing remark about *Off to See the Lizard* in the *Rolling Stone Record Guide.*

A37. c

A38. d

A39. b. Yup, believe it or not, that's none other than Elvis's very own Jordanaires singing along with the hiccuping Jimmy Buffett. As for a, I have no idea where I came up with that name.

A40. b. Max Bialystock (d) is a character played by Zero Mostel in the movie *The Producers.* Buffett mentions Bialystock in the playbill for *Don't Stop the Carnival.*

A41. *A Tennessee Christmas*

A42. The Islander. It was on Boca Chica Key, which lies just east of Key West.

A43. Michael Utley

A44. ALL of them were written by Wouk. This time, it's all or nothing. If you said all five, take 5 points. If you said anything else, take nothing.

A45. c

A46. a

A47. a. Before they disbanded, Shakoor was a member of the rap/dance group Arrested Development. The name of Buffett's other vocalists are Claudia Cummings, Tina Gullickson, and Nicky Yarling (who doubles on violin).

A48. c. Aaron Neville didn't participate in the project, but I imagine that he would have been a good choice for the project, with his falsetto swirling around Sinatra's deepened baritone. Bono (a) and Kenny G (e) appeared on Volume I, while Willie Nelson (b) and Chrissie Hynde (d) appeared on Volume II.

A49. a, b, d, and e are correct. c and f are from *South Pacific.* 5 points for all four, or 1 point each.

A50. a. I *really, really* hope that you wouldn't have picked e.

A51. d. Believe me or not, "A Pirate Looks at Forty" was culled as a single but never even scraped onto *Billboard's Hot 100*.

A52. c. Although the A-side did nothing chartwise, "Door Number Three" did appear briefly on *Billboard*'s Country chart at no. 88.

A53. a. John Sebastian, late of the Lovin' Spoonful

A54. b. Alex Harvey, late of the Sensational Alex Harvey Band

A55. c. Roger Bartlett, late of the Coral Reefer Band

A56. d. Jimmy Buffett, not much late of (or for) anything. I figured that I might have tricked you with this one coming after the previous few questions. Did I?

A57. e. Fingers Taylor. It's a good thing he plays harmonica as well as he does, isn't it?

A58. "...they'd look a lot better as beer cans" (from "Migration)

A59. "...or east of Pensacola" (from "Life is Just a Tire Swing")

A60. "...and Monty I sure need the dough." (from "Door Number Three"—Monty, by the way, is game-show host Monty Hall)

A61. Fooled ya!! At least I think I did. You picked *Changes in Latitudes, Changes in Attitudes*, didn't you? Well, that album features a completed version of the song, but the revised title is "Wonder *Why* We Ever Go Home." "Wonder Why *You* Ever go Home" appeared on the *Rancho Deluxe Soundtrack*.

A62. a

A63. d. In "Migration," he sings about getting a sweat-stained Bogart suit, an African parakeet, and moving down to Martinique when he becomes an old man.

A64. Paris

A65. "In the Shelter," "Livingston's Gone to Texas," and "The Captain and the Kid."

A66. c

A67. "...but that's been gone since early this morn'."

A68. "Margaritaville"

A69. "...and I feel like I'm pullin' a trailer."

A70. "Son of a Son of a Sailor"

A71. "...and get drunk on cheap-ass beer."

A72. "Miss You So Badly"

A73. "eighty-sixed," as in kicked out

A74. from "Cliches"

A75. "Ecuador"

A76. "Havana Daydreamin' "

A77. "stewardess"

A78. "Weather is Here, Wish You Were Beautiful"

A79. b. Although all might bear some vague resemblance, only in "The Weather is Here, Wish You Were Beautiful" does the main character decide to blow off his life in New York for the Caribbean.

A80. a and b. Take 1 point for one and 5 for both. Don't take nothin' if you chose c, d or e, though.

A81. b

A82. 2. "Margaritaville," 3. "Come Monday," and 4. "A Pirate Looks at Forty."

A83. a

A84. d ("Mea culpa, mea culpa, mea maxima culpa"). This was spoken as an act of contrition, admitting sins committed (or otherwise, since "natural" sin came into play as well).

A85. "Overkill." This rhyme scheme crops up in the form of a rap, something that I wouldn't have expected from Buffett in three lifetimes.

A86. "Love in the Library."

A87. "Fruitcakes" and "Desdemona's Building a Rocket Ship." Take 2 points if you could only name one, 5 points otherwise.

A88. d. The live version of "God's Own Drunk" from *You Had to Be There* clocks in at 10:45, and that's not counting the 2:04 spoken introduction. For what it's worth, Buffett's longest studio recording is "False Echoes," reaching 9:14. Allowing for the fact that you might not have considered live recordings, I'll give two points if you chose f. Other than live recordings, Buffett's work before 1990 rarely strayed over five minutes in length—"Creola" was his personal "best," reaching 7:00 even in length. Since then, long songs have been the rule more than the exception; "Fruitcakes" reaches 7:40, "Everybody's Got a Cousin in Miami" is 7:19 and "Desdemona's Building a Rocket Ship" is 7:05.

A89. Anson Funderburgh and the Rockets

A90. Three are originals; "A Sailor's Christmas," "Ho Ho Ho and a Bottle of Rhum," and "Merry Christmas, Alabama." Take 2 points if you said there were three originals, and add 1 point for each that you were able to name.

A92. a. The events described in "False Echoes" take place on the 25th of November, 1921—his dad's first birthday.

A93. a-4, b-2, c-6, d-5, e-1, f-3.

A94. a-3, b-1, c-5, d-2, e-4.

A95. a-3, b-5, c-2, d-1, e-4.

A96. a-2, b-6, c-4, d-5, e-1, f-3.

A97. "Why Don't We Get Lunch at School"

A98. "Abandoned on Tuesday" b/w "Don't Bring Me Candy." On Buffett's recent summer tour, he plays a game where audience members attempt to stump the band by requesting obscure songs. One clever wise guy tripped up Buffett and Coral Reefers by requesting "Abandoned on Tuesday." You couldn't have gotten this right, could you?

A99. "Stars Fell on Alabama." It was published in 1934. The reason for the disclaimer in the question was because "Goodnight Irene," which is older than dirt, appeared on one of the Margaritaville compilations. If you guessed "On a Slow Boat to China," then you were close—Buffett was not yet two years old when this song was published in 1948—so I'll give you 2 points.

A100. James Taylor and his son, Ben.

EXTRA CREDIT STUFF

No. 1. Buffett's sports jersey is No. 22 and a replica is available in the *Coconut Telegraph*.

No. 2. Buffett's "Great Eight," the eight songs that he considers to be "must-do's" and rarely skips during a typical full-length performance, are

1. "Why Don't We Get Drunk"
2. "Come Monday"
3. "Margaritaville"
4. "Changes in Latitudes, Changes in Attitudes"
5. "Son of a Son of a Sailor"
6. "Cheeseburger in Paradise"
7. "Volcano"
8. "Fins"

So, how'd you do?

0–200 points—Oops. Sorry 'bout that, but don't say that I didn't warn you. So, maybe you're factual retention is a bit skewed, or maybe you just don't *care* about this trivial stuff. You're still a fan, right? All right, I believe you. If you want to be a Parrot Head, you're a Parrot Head. It's as simple as that. See, you didn't even have to take this dumb quiz (*now* I tell you).

201–399 points—So what's it like to be stuck in the middle with everybody else? No, I didn't expect you to do any better, but anybody who would sit down and subject themselves to 501 grueling questions about their favorite artist is okay in my book. You never would have done this otherwise, and you didn't even do half-bad, so guess what? YOU'RE A PARROT HEAD!

400–500—Not for nothing, but don't you think you ought to put this book down and get back to work on rocket science? Well, you did it. I don't know how, but you did it. I wasn't even going to write anything here, assuming that nobody would score this high anyway, and...Hey, wait a minute! You're not Jimmy Buffett, are you? Just checking. Well, if he ever contacts me looking for some bizarrely inane factual tidbit about his life, maybe I can give him your name and number, because I've had enough trivia for a while. Congratulations on your dedicated insanity, Parrot Head. May the next trivia book be all yours.

SEE THAT??!! EVERYBODY'S A PARROT HEAD!!!!

ACKNOWLEDGMENTS

Special thanks to my family (extended or otherwise), especially Robin, Dare, and Kyle; Laura Tucker; Rob Clark and Wes Schroeppel, for supplying me with every scrap of info that they possessed concerning the Head Parrot; Beth Altamira, for keeping track of said Head Parrot's whereabouts in the news; Chris Markferding, Scott Henderson, Tom Liddle, Bill Lack, Scott Nickerson, and the other cyber-people who offered me assitance; Steve Beery and the staff at Mr. Meery's; The Smoky Mountain Parrot Head Club members; the Nashville Parrot Head Club members; the Atlanta Parrot Head Club members; Sue (for the convertible), Mike (for the inside scoop), Steve (for wearing a hula skirt in public), and the dozens of other mega-fans that I met during my time in Knoxville who were willing to share their stories with me.